HORRIBLE HISTORIES

TWO HORRIBLE BOOKS IN ONE

THE SMASHING SAXONS

AND

THE STORMIN' NORMANS

Terry Deary ✺ Martin Brown

SCHOLASTIC

Scholastic Children's Books
Euston House
24 Eversholt Street
London
NW1 1DB
UK

A division of Scholastic Ltd
London ~ New York ~ Toronto ~ Sydney ~ Auckland
Mexico City ~ New Delhi ~ Hong Kong

Published in this edition by Scholastic Ltd, 2006
Cover illustration copyright © Martin Brown, 2002

The Smashing Saxons
First published in the UK by Scholastic Ltd, 2000
Text copyright © Terry Deary, 2000
Illustrations copyright © Martin Brown, 2000

The Stormin' Normans
First published in the UK by Scholastic Ltd, 2001
Text copyright © Terry Deary, 2001
Illustrations copyright © Martin Brown, 2001

10 digit ISBN: 0 439 95939 X
13 digit ISBN: 978 0439 95939 1

Contents

The Smashing Saxons

The Stormin' Normans

THE SMASHING
SAXONS

For George Barron, with thanks.

Introduction

History can be horrible. Especially those history lessons where the teacher asks impossible questions. You know the sort of thing …

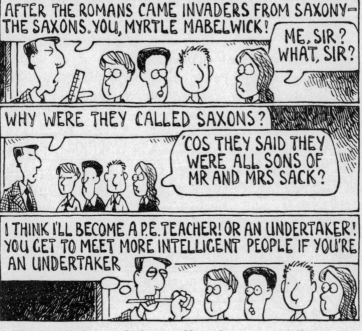

Forget all the confusing stuff teachers try to tell you …

'Saxon' was a name the Welsh, the Scots and the Irish called all the strangers who moved into England when the Romans left. Just tell your teacher: 'It was never that simple. Let's just use the word "Saxon" the way they meant it. Saxons were the people who invaded the place we now call England.'

And don't worry … there is an escape from the terrible tortures of teachers asking questions.

It's time for pupil power and for biting back! Now, with the help of a *Horrible Histories* book, you can turn the tables on teachers. Now *you* can ask the questions!

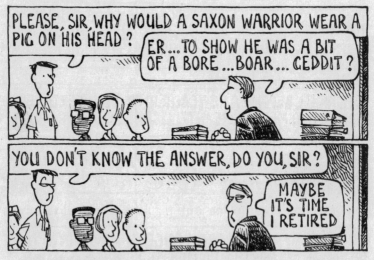

Knowledge is power, see? Now you can find out fascinating facts, like what a whip made from the skin of a dolphin would be used for, and then test your teacher.

By the time you've finished the teacher may need that whip. Why? Read on …

Timeline

410 After 300 years the Romans in Britain go back to Rome. The Brits have to fight off powerful Picts, savage Scots and invading Irish raiders.

449 The Brits hire a couple of bothersome Saxon brothers from Jutland, Hengest and Horsa, to fight for them. H & H like it so much they decided to stay, batter the Brits and settle. There's gratitude for you!

460s The Brits fight back against the Saxons under a leader called Ambrosius and about twenty years later a warrior called Arthur takes over. That's not the legendary bloke with a round table. This King Arthur was probably the last great Roman British leader.

491 The Saxon leader Aelle (call him 'Ella') becomes the first ruler of a South Saxon kingdom. He attacks British defenders at the old Roman fortress in Pevensey and massacres the lot of them.

511 Brit hero King Arthur dies (probably) at the battle of Camlann. The Brits will struggle hopelessly now he's gone.

597 Christian missionaries arrive from Rome and Saxons are

converted – mostly. (Some go back to being pagans later. Maybe it's more fun.)

600s The Saxons gradually take over the land we now call England with the Northumbrian kingdom in the north, the Mercians in the middle, the Anglians in the East and the kingdom of Wessex in the south. Very neat, very cosy.

787 Mercian leader King Offa is so powerful he can organize the digging of a 20-metre-wide ditch between England and Wales, 169 miles (270 km) long to keep the wild Welsh away. His ditch is known as Offa's Dyke.

793 The Vikings are coming from Norway. Bad news for savaged Saxons and massacred monks. These are just raids – later they'll be back to stay.

871 Alfred the Great becomes king of Wessex and defeats and drives back the vicious Vikings from the south of England. But they don't go home. They stay in the north and the east. Alfie may be 'Great' but he hasn't vanquished the Vikings really.

924 Alf's grandson, Athelstan, avoids a plot to blind him and becomes king. He's a real 'great'

even though he's usually forgotten. He's the man to sort out the Vikings, not to mention the Welsh and the Scots. Wessex are winners! Britain is a single Saxon country for the first time. But not for long …

937 The Welsh, Scots, Irish and Vikings all gang up to rebel and destroy Athelstan. He and his Saxons beat them in a bloody battle at Brunanburh – probably in Yorkshire.

939 Athelstan dies. Guess what? The Vikings are back, led by Olaf Guthfrithsson who takes over as king in the north. He means trouble.

978 Saxon King Edward the Martyr is murdered. Ethelred the Unready (his step-brother) takes the crown. But did Eth have something to do with the death? Eth tries to pay the Vikings to go away – giving them gold weighing 10,000 kilos in 991 – so they keep coming back! Who can blame them?

1002 King Ethelred organizes a massacre of the Viking settlers – the women and children and the defenceless farmers, because they don't fight back! But the Viking warriors will avenge them.

1012 Now poor old Eth gives the greedy Vikings 20,000 kilos of gold

to go away. It does him (and the English) no good because …

1013 Ethelred is driven off the throne and replaced by invading Viking Sweyn. Eth runs off to Normandy till Sweyn dies. Eth tries a bit of a comeback but then Sweyn's son Cnut returns and sees him off.

1042 Edward the Confessor becomes king. He gets a bit too friendly with the Normans.

1066 …and that's that! Last Saxon king, Harold, is defeated by William the Conqueror and his Normans.

The Saxon start

Battering the Brits

Have you ever noticed how school books *tell* you things but they never seem to answer the questions you want to ask. But this is a *Horrible Histories* book, so now's your chance to quiz the author. Well? What are you waiting for?

WHO WERE THESE SAXON PEOPLE?

Well they came from North Germany and invaded Britain from about AD 300 onwards. They liked it so much they stayed.

SO WHAT WAS WRONG WITH NORTH GERMANY THEN?

A lot of them lived on little islands surrounded by marsh or sea. Terrible farming land, so they went off and pinched someone else's.

DID NO ONE TRY TO STOP THEM?

Of course they did! The Romans who ran Britain stopped them. Then, when the Romans left, the Brits tried to stop them.

BUT THE SAXONS WON?

They drove the Brits west into Wales and Cornwall. Then the Vikings came across and tried to push the Saxons out.

SERVES THEM RIGHT! SO WHY ISN'T ENGLAND CALLED SAXONLAND?

Just one of those things. It was the Welsh and the Scots and the Irish who called them Saxons. By about 800, the Saxons were calling themselves 'Anglisc' – their spelling wasn't as good as yours.

OK, WHERE DID THE SAXONS GO?

Nowhere. They stayed in Britain. But in 1066 the Normans came across and took control. The Normans became the rulers and the Saxons became the peasants. Today's British people are a mixture of Saxon and Norman and lots of others.

SO WHAT KIND OF PEOPLE WERE THESE SAXONS?

That would take a whole book to answer.

BOOKS ARE BORING!

Horrible Histories aren't.

SO WHERE CAN I FIND A HORRIBLE HISTORY OF THE SAXONS?

You're reading it, stupid!

OOOOH! SO I AM!

Horrible Hengest

In the 420s the Brits were led by Vortigern.

HERE! I SAY, YOU CHAPS! THAT WASN'T MY *NAME* YOU KNOW! VORTIGERN WAS MY *TITLE* AND IT MEANS 'GREAT KING'. JOLLY GOOD TITLE TOO!

Vortigern led the Brits from about AD 425 till 450. He organized the Brits after the Roman armies left and his real name may have been Vitalinus – which sounds a bit like a medicine.

But Vortigern had problems, as we know from a horrible history written by a priest and historian called Gildas, who was writing almost a hundred years after Vortigern ruled.

The feathered flight of a rumour reached the ears of everyone in south Britain. Their old enemies from the north were on their way. They weren't coming to raid but to rule the country from end to end. But before they could defend themselves they rushed down that wide road that leads to death. A deadly plague killed so many and so quickly that there weren't enough left alive to bury the dead ...

What did the Brits do when peppered by plague and Picts?

So what did Vortigern do? Gildas said Vortigern's council 'went blind'. What he *meant* was they couldn't see how stupid their actions were ...

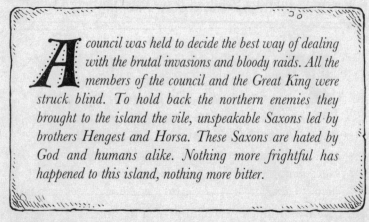

A council was held to decide the best way of dealing with the brutal invasions and bloody raids. All the members of the council and the Great King were struck blind. To hold back the northern enemies they brought to the island the vile, unspeakable Saxons led by brothers Hengest and Horsa. These Saxons are hated by God and humans alike. Nothing more frightful has happened to this island, nothing more bitter.

Do you get the feeling that Gildas didn't like the Saxons?

He went on to curse Vortigern and the council …

> *What utter blindness of their wits. What raw, hopeless stupidity!*

Sounds a bit like my teacher when he read my history homework!

Anyway, Vortigern paid the warrior-bullies Hengest and Horsa to fight for him …

AND THE BOYS DONE WELL

…but then the Saxon visitors turned nasty and demanded a lump of Brit land for themselves. One hundred years later, Gildas was still furious at Vortigern's stupidity …

> *Vortigern's council invited an enemy under their own roof that they feared more than death. These Saxons fixed their claws on the eastern coast, as if they planned to defend it. When they were settled they invited friends to join them. For a long time the Britons gave them supplies to 'shut the dog's mouth'.*

But the Saxon 'dogs' were hungry. The more they got the more they wanted and they were ready to fight for it.

Vortigern's plan worked for a little while and the Picts and Irish were held back. The *Kentish Chronicle* history makes it sound pathetic …

> The Saxon barbarians grew in number. They demanded the food and clothing that Vortigern promised but the Britons said, 'We cannot feed and clothe you, for your numbers are grown. Go away, for we do not need your help.'

Imagine being in the Brits' position. You ask the school bully to help you. He turns on you and demands your school dinner money. And you say, 'Go away, for I do not need your help!' Think it would work?

Hah! No way. And it didn't work for the Britons. But then another Roman Briton called Ambrosius rebelled against Vortigern. Who did Vortigern turn to for help to fight Ambrosius?

MY BRAVE SAXON CHUMS OF COURSE. NATURALLY OLD HENGEST TOLD ME HE DIDN'T HAVE ENOUGH FIGHTING FELLOWS TO BATTLE AGAINST ALL OF AMBROSIUS' AWFUL MEN. HE WANTED TO FETCH ANOTHER TWENTY BOATLOADS OF HIS SAXON MATES ACROSS

Hengest didn't just bring more warriors. He brought a secret weapon: his daughter! The old historian describes what happened next ...

> *In one of the ships was Hengest's daughter, a very beautiful girl. Hengest arranged a feast for Vortigern and his soldiers. They got very drunk and the Devil entered into Vortigern's heart, making him fall in love with the girl. He asked Hengest for her hand in marriage and said, 'I will give anything you want in return – even half my kingdom!'*

Of course it wasn't Vortigern's kingdom to give away! The land belonged to the dukes who ruled each county. But Vortigern gave Hengest the county of Kent – without even asking the Kent lord Gwyrangon.

In around AD 449, from his new base in Kent, Hengest was ready to take over Britain and he didn't care how much blood was spilled. Gildas said ...

> *All the great towns fell to the Saxon battering rams. Bishops, priests and people were all chopped down together while swords flashed and flames crackled. It was horrible to see the stones of towers thrown down to mix with pieces of human bodies. Broken altars were covered with a purple crust of clotted blood. There was no burial except under ruins and bodies were eaten by the birds and beasts.*

Horrible history! But a bit over the top. Modern historians don't think the Saxon rebellion was all that bloody and violent.

Anyway, the Brits fought back …

I SENT MY OWN SON, VORTEMIR, OFF TO FIGHT OLD HENGEST. YOU KNOW, HE WHIPPED THE SAXONS LIKE DOGS AND KILLED OLD HENGEST'S BROTHER HORSA. I THINK THE SAVAGE SAXONS GOT MY MESSAGE: YOU DON'T MESS WITH VORTIGERN

Then young Vortemir was killed. The Saxons came back with a really 'vile, unspeakable' plot. If Vortigern had left a diary it might have looked something like this …

24th August, St Bartholomew's Day, AD 456

Oh dear!
Oh dear, oh dear!
Oh dear, oh dear, oh dear!
Those frightfully nice Saxon chappies have turned out to be simply… well, frightful. It was bad enough their killing poor little Vortemir but now they've turned nasty.

That Hengest bloke (who smells a little, to be honest) invited us over to talk about peace and one thought it was a jolly good idea, don't you know. After all, I'm married to his lovely daughter, so he wouldn't harm me. 'Bring along your top generals, no weapons though,' he said. 'We'll have a bit of a party — some ale, a few nibbles and a jolly sing song!' It sounded just like the good old days when the Saxon blokes first came over.

In fact it all sounded jolly jolly. 'When would you like us to come over?' one asked.

'Saint Bartholomew's Eve — seven thirty for eight,' he said.

'Topping!' one replied. 'See you then, old boy.'

Oh dear, oh, dear. The clue was there, wasn't it? Saint Bartholomew was that missionary chappie who went to Africa to convert the pagans. They skinned him alive and chopped his head off. So one ought to have guessed that it wasn't a good evening to meet the jolly old pagan enemy.

Sure enough I arrived with all the top chaps in Britain — my best warriors, best ministers and the best bishops. What did the savage Saxons do? Why they sat us down at the tables, waited till we were munching on the jolly old nibbles and then Hengest cried out, 'Saxons! Draw your knives!' They jolly well drew their dirty great knives that they'd hidden in their boots! Not very sporting. In fact it's cheating, don't you think?

Chop! Chop! Chop! It was over in seconds — well, actually we didn't have any seconds. They killed the chaps while they were eating their firsts! Blood all over the tables. Blood all over the rushes on the floor. Someone's going to have a sticky, messy, job cleaning that up one can jolly well tell you! The only one they left alive was me. One has to go back and tell the British chaps that 'Hengest rules OK!' Since one has lost all one's top chappies one doesn't have a lot of choice, does one?

I'm a prisoner and I had to give horrible Hengest quite a lot of land just to spare my life.
Oh dear!
Oh dear, oh dear!
Oh dear, oh dear, oh dear!

What happened to Vortigern? He survived but was hated by everyone. In the end …

Vortigern wandered from place to place till his heart broke and he died without honour.

Gildas the writer was trying to explain what a dreadful place Britain was and how it had been better in the good old Roman days. Maybe he made the Saxon rebellion sound worse than it was. Archaeologists have dug on a lot of Saxon and British sites and they can't find much proof that this violent rebellion ever happened.

But, violent or peaceful, the Saxons had arrived and they meant to stay.

Superstitious Saxons

The Dark Ages are a bit of a mystery to us – that's how they got their name. But they were also really dark! After the sun set there were no streetlights to show the way. Only moonlight, starlight and some whacking great scary shadows.

So it's no wonder the Saxons believed all sorts of weird and horrible things went on in those shadows. Devils and demons lurked there, ready to snatch your soul and carry it off to Hell!

EVEN THOUGH I SAY IT MYSELF, IF THERE'S ONE THING I DO RATHER WELL, IT'S LURK

You believed in charms and spells to protect you. You became superstitious – especially about how you buried your dead.

Dead losses

In the early days, before they became Christian, the Saxons would sometimes bury a servant with his (or her) dead master. The servant would then be able to serve the master in the afterlife. But the horrible historical fact is the servant was often buried alive! They were thrown into the open grave, a heavy stone may have been thrown on top to keep them down and then they were covered with soil.

If it wasn't a servant then it was some poor woman, buried alive to keep the man company in the afterlife – cook his dinner, wash his clothes and polish his sword. It seems that

24

even in the afterlife men were hopeless!

Even dogs were sacrificed to go with their masters to the afterlife. What would dogs *do* there? Are there any trees for pees in heaven?

The Saxons brought a lot of their funeral habits with them from Europe. Then, in AD 597 St Augustine arrived in southern England to convert the Saxons to Christianity. When the Saxons became Christian there was a mixture of old customs and new ones ... and some customs you wouldn't want to happen to your worst enemy or even your history teacher ...

A pane in the ash
Saxons were worried about the ghosts of the dead coming back to haunt them.

Would you worry about your dead Auntie Ethelburga coming back to haunt you? Then here are a few helpful early-Saxon hints ...

1 Cremate her. When early Saxons cremated a dead friend they would place the ashes in a small jar or urn. Then they would leave a small window in the jar. Why? So the spirit could come and go and not make trouble if it found its ashes trapped in a sealed container.

MIND YOU, WINDOWS DO HAVE THEIR DISADVANTAGES

I CAN SEEEEE YOU!

2 Cut her head off. The living dead find it a bit hard to haunt without a head. They wouldn't even find their way out of the burial yard. So lop off their dead head and save yourself from a haunting.

3 Give her some company. Sometimes there were the ashes of more than one person in a pot. Auntie Ethelburga will be so busy gossiping to her powdered pal that she'll forget to haunt you.

4 Give her some treasure. The dead are happy if they are buried with some of their precious possessions. Women could be buried with jewellery like dress fasteners. A man might be buried with a sword or throwing spear. (He's bound to be a dead shot.)

5 Burn crops. Garlic keeps vampires away, they say, and the Saxons believed burning crops kept ghosts away. (Do *not* try this with your breakfast cornflakes. Especially after your

26

mum's poured milk over them). This useful trick was banned by boring Archbishop Theodore in AD 672.

WHY WASTE WORTHWHILE WHEAT WHEN WE WANT WICKEDNESS WITHDRAWN?

It's just as well the Saxons had these ghost-busting ideas because there were a lot of dead people around. Half of them were dead before they reached 25 years old and not many of the rest reached 40.

Good god

When the Saxons first came to Britain they were 'pagans' – they worshipped German gods like …

GODS

Name: Tiw
Day to remember: Tuesday named after him.
Top job: God of 'Justice'.
Foul fact: He allowed himself to be used as the bait to trap a monstrous wolf. The wolf bit his hand off. Don't try this at home. (Maybe he should also be the god of stupidity.)

Name: Woden

Day to remember: Wednesday named after him.

Top job: The top god and god of poets.

Foul fact: He owned an eight-legged horse (must have cost a fortune in horse-shoes) that could fly through the air. He swapped one of his eyes for wisdom – don't try this at school.

Name: Thunor

Day to remember: Thursday named after him.

Top job: God of thunder.

Foul fact: Had a magic throwing hammer that came back to him like a boomerang. (Don't try this in the park.) Incredibly strong but has so far failed to smash the skull of the serpent of evil. He'll do it at Ragnarok – that's the end of the worlds of gods and humans.

Name: Frigg

Day to remember: Friday named after her.

Top job: Woden's wife – goddess of marriage.

Foul fact: She didn't lose an eye or a hand but she did lose her son, Balder, who was killed with the only thing that could harm him – mistletoe. (So watch what you stand under next Christmas!)

Although the Saxons later converted to being Christians they kept bits of their old religion in their religious ceremonies. They were a mixture of Christian and pagan – maybe they believed the Christian God and the pagan gods would work together for better effect!

Foul fields

Do you have a field that has been cursed? Maybe a school football field where you always seem to lose? Why not get your head teacher to try this ancient Saxon cure?

FIRST CUT FOUR SQUARES OF TURF FROM EACH CORNER OF THE FIELD. WATCH OUT FOR THOSE WORMS!

MIX OIL, HONEY, YEAST, MILK, SAWDUST AND HOLY WATER. THEN SPRINKLE THE MIXTURE ON TO THE UNDERSIDE OF THE TURF – GIVE THOSE WORMS A BATH

YUM!

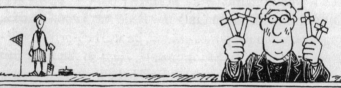

SEND FOR YOUR PRIEST WHO MUST MAKE FOUR CROSSES FROM POPLAR WOOD – OR A COUPLE OF LOLLY STICKS MAY DO THE TRICK

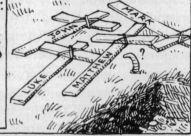

WRITE A NAME ON EACH: MATTHEW, MARK, LUKE AND JOHN. PLACE THE CROSSES IN THE HOLES LEFT WHERE YOU REMOVED THE TURF AND HOPE THE WORMS AREN'T TOO CROSS

MARK
JOHN
LUKE
MATTHEW
?

THE PRIEST MUST THEN BOW NINE TIMES TO THE EAST AND TURN NINE TIMES CLOCKWISE BEFORE PUTTING THE TURFS BACK. BET THE WORMS ARE GLAD TO BE HOME

If all that doesn't make you win you could always try an ancient pagan practice and sacrifice the referee.

Did you know … ?
Even though the historian Saint Bede was a good Christian, and believed in the power of God, he also believed a lot of the superstitions of the Saxon people – and so did most of the Christians who lived at the time. He believed that God sent messages to people on earth through his miracles … and also through strange signs.

In the year 729 Bede reported that there were two comets seen in the skies. He said this was a heavenly sign that a disaster was going to happen. In fact an army from Asia attacked France and caused a lot of death and destruction to Christians there.

In 734 there were reports that the moon turned the colour of blood and blood rained down from the skies – shortly afterwards Bede died!

What other odd ideas did the Saxons have … ?

Wacky weather wisdom

The Saxons watched out for signs for their weather forecasts – but signs didn't just foretell the weather! What did these signs mean?

Sign	Meaning
1. Thunder on a Sunday means...	a)...gale-force winds will follow
2. Dolphins leaping from the water means...	b)...calm weather will follow
3. Thunder on a Wednesday means...	c)...the death of nuns and monks
4. Red sky at night means...	d)...there will be a storm
5. Splashes from oars glittering on a night voyage means...	e)...the death of lazy women

Answers: 1c); 2a); 3e); 4b); 5d).

32

Sutton who?

In 1939 some archaeologists began digging into a Saxon burial mound. It was at a place called Sutton Hoo, not far from the town of Ipswich in East Anglia, and the site turned out to be a great discovery.

But sixty years later no one can quite agree what they uncovered. It was a 24 metre wooden ship from around the year AD 600, buried with treasure in memory of a great person. There were over 40 gold items and a great silver dish. Most historians agree on that … but not much else. For example, there was an iron stand found in the grave. They argue it was either …

- a torch holder
- a standard (sort of a flag-pole) for soldiers to follow
- or a rack to show off the scalps of dead enemies!

HAS ANYONE SEEN MY SPEAR FRAME?

33

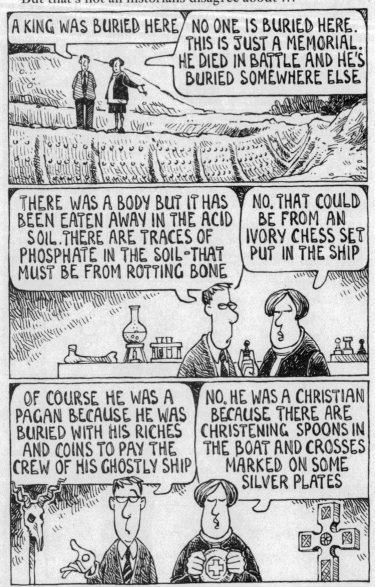

Was there ever a body in the boat?

Archaeologists and scientists looked at soil samples and grave goods for forty years and couldn't agree. Then, in 1979, they decided to look at the notes made by the first diggers. And they made an amazing discovery. There in the notes was one line no one had noticed before …

Complete set of iron coffin fittings arranged in a rectangle

There *had* been a coffin after all! So it's pretty certain there was a body in the grave! What happened to these important clues, the coffin fittings?

Hoo knows? They are missing.

Did you know … ?
Some Saxon helmets had a wild pig on top. No! Not a real one, dummy. A little metal model.

WHY DID SAXON HELMETS HAVE PIGS ON ?

I'm glad you asked me that.

The pig was sacred to the god of peace, Frey, and the goddess of battle and death, his sister Freyja. The pig was a good luck sign!

Next time you have a school exam or a SAT test, why not try wearing a wild pig on your head?

WILL A SLICE OF BACON BRING ME A SLICE OF LUCK ?

Awesome Arthur

The years from about AD 450 till around 500 were the darkest years of the Dark Ages.

Battered Brits bite back

Luckily the priest Gildas gives us a horrible historical idea of what it was like then for the poor old Brits …

> *Some of the wretched British were caught in the hills and slaughtered in heaps. Some gave themselves up as slaves. Some hid in the thick forests and the cliffs, terrified, until the savage Saxon raiders went home again.*

The Saxons were battering the Brits, but some Brits started fighting back. They wanted a Britain the way it was in the old Roman days of eighty years before. One leader managed to win forty years of peace. He was called 'the last Roman' and his name was Arthur.

Five hundred years after Arthur died his name was remembered and storytellers came up with some great tales of Arthur's deeds. In a word they were bosh. In four words they were total and utter bosh. Any historian will tell you …

Happy History for Cute Kids

- King Arthur pulled a magical sword from a stone. *Bosh!*

- Arthur was given his war sword, Excalibur, by the Lady of the Lake. *Tosh!*

- Arthur gathered his knights at a round table at the wonderful palace of Camelot. *Piffle!*

- Arthur and his knights fought against evil in their shining armour. *Twaddle!*

- Arthur was betrayed by the wicked Mordred and beaten in battle. *Tommyrot!*

- Now Arthur is lying asleep and he will awaken and return when Britain is in danger. *Tripe!*

The truth is there are very few clues as to who Arthur was, what he did, or even where he lived and fought. A monk called Nennius wrote of twelve battles that Arthur fought in.

The twelfth battle was on Badon Hill where 960 men fell in one day from one attack by Arthur. No one killed them but he alone.

Arthur killed 960 Saxons by himself! What? His little arms must have been aching!

Nennius was writing a couple of hundred years after Arthur died. He probably copied the battle list from an old Welsh battle poem. The trouble is those poems exaggerate just a bit to make their heroes sound like Superman. The truth is (probably) that he was from a Roman family, and led the Brits so well that the Saxons were held back in the south and east of England for forty years.

What story books and history books don't tell you is that the King Arthur from the oldest legends wasn't a goody-goody leader fighting against evil. Arthur could be pretty awful!

Awful Arthur

How about hearing some of the stories about the awful side of Arthur … ?

Once upon a time, in the middle of Wales, there was a tyrant who came from foreign parts and his name was Arthur. When this Arthur came to the monastery at Llanbadarn Fawr he met the bishop Paternus and he cast his eyes greedily on the bishop's fine tunic. 'Bishop!' said Arthur. 'That is a wonderful tunic and I want it for my own!'

And the bishop replied, 'This tunic is for priests! A wicked man may not wear it, and you are a wicked man.'

Then Arthur fell into a mighty rage and left the monastery, raving furiously. Later that day he returned and found bishop Paternus praying.

Arthur snatched at the bishop's tunic and tried to tear it off him. Arthur cursed and Arthur swore in the sight of God. Arthur stamped on the ground like a child.

Then bishop Paternus said, 'Let the earth swallow him up!'

The earth at once opened in a great crack and swallowed Arthur up to the chin. The wicked king was afraid and begged, 'Forgive me please, Paternus. Forgive me!'

Bishop Paternus, the saint, forgave the greedy king and at once the crack in the earth spewed King Arthur up.

And Arthur was *not* a friend to ladies in distress …

One day cruel King Arthur was riding with three of his knights when he saw a woman carried on a horse by a man. A troop of soldiers were chasing them.

'Look, Arthur! That lady is being chased by those soldiers! We should help her to escape!' the knights cried.

But when wicked Arthur saw the woman his heart was filled with desire and he wanted her for himself. 'No, my knights!' he cried. 'Take the woman and bring her to me! She's just the sort of lady that I could take for my love!'

'You can't do that!' his knights said.

'I can! I'm king!' the angry Arthur argued.

'We have to help the lady!' the knights said angrily.

Arthur scowled and Arthur fretted and then he said, 'Oh, very well. If you would rather help a lady than grab the girl for me, then go ahead.'

And so the knights rode down and saved the lady and they gave her their protection.

But Arthur, he was not a happy king.

Then there's the idea that Arthur was a 'religious' king who fought under the Christian cross against the pagan Saxons.

At the battle of Badon Arthur carried the cross of our Lord Jesus Christ on his shoulders for three days and nights and the Britons won victory.

This is the battle where he slew 960 Saxons single handed … with a cross on his back! Did he use the cross to batter the 960 to death? Whew! What a man!

But hang on … another old story says he took the altar from a church and used it to eat his dinner! Would a good Christian do that? So much for a knight of the round table – he was more like a knight of the nicked table.

And what would the noble Arthur do to a brave enemy? Spare his life and make him a friend? No chance …

41

In farthest Scotland was a warrior prince and this man's name was Cuill. Now Cuill was a brave warrior and a famous soldier who bowed down to no king, not even Arthur.

He would often come down from Scotland, burning and raiding and winning great victories. And Arthur, the king of all Britain, heard what this gallant young man was doing. Many people hoped Cuill would take Arthur's place one day, but Arthur sought him out and murdered him.

After the murder Arthur went home, feeling very happy to have killed such a strong enemy.

So there you have another view of Arthur. Thief and murderer with no respect for women or the Church. These story writers were writing long after Arthur's death, but it's interesting that, at the time, no one argued with the way they described him – as a wicked man. Take your pick:

THE GREAT ARTHUR DEBATE

BRAVE RESPECTED HERO	GREEDY CRUEL VILLAIN	NOBLE GOD-FEARING KNIGHT	STORY-BOOK LEGEND
BRITISH MONK AD 540	WELSH POET AD 1000	NORMAN MONK AD 1300	HISTORIAN AD 2000

We'll probably never know the whole truth now. Arthur can be whatever you want him to be.

Naughty nuns and mischievous monks

If you were a Christian Saxon peasant you could escape from the pain of the plough and the foulness of the farm by joining a monastery. The monasteries encouraged parents to send their sons at the age of seven. But it would cost them …

Making monks

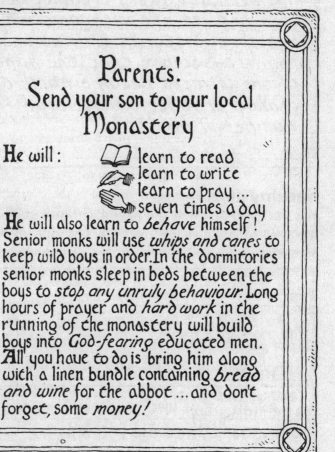

Parents!
Send your son to your local Monastery

He will:
- learn to read
- learn to write
- learn to pray … seven times a day

He will also learn to *behave* himself! Senior monks will use *whips and canes* to keep wild boys in order. In the dormitories senior monks sleep in beds between the boys to *stop any unruly behaviour.* Long hours of prayer and *hard work* in the running of the monastery will build boys into *God-fearing* educated men. **All** you have to do is bring him along with a linen bundle containing *bread and wine* for the abbot … and don't forget, some *money!*

What they didn't mention was that life could be hard. The Abbot of Monkwearmouth, a monastery in north-eastern England, wrote a letter to a friend in Germany and said:

> During the past winter our island has been savagely troubled with cold and ice and with long and widespread storms of wind and rain. It is so bad that the hands of the writers become numb and cannot produce a very large number of books.

Naughty nuns

You worked and prayed and prayed and worked. You were supposed to lead a simple, holy life, but many monks and nuns enjoyed life a bit more than they were supposed to.

Some Saxon letters have survived with complaints a bit like this one …

> My dear abbess,
>
> I was shocked and horrified on my visit to your convent. I expected to see holy women, simply and modestly dressed. What did I find?

> × Nuns who crimped their hair with
>   curling irons.
> × Nuns wearing brightly coloured
>   head-dresses laced with ribbons
>   down to their ankles.
> × Nuns with sharpened fingernails
>   like hawks' talons.
> I hope these disgraceful practices
> will cease immediately.
>   Angry from Tunbridge Wells

And many monks were no better. The monk–historian Bede told the story of Coldingham monastery in Northumbria:

> The cells that were built for praying were turned into places of feasting and drinking.

A Celt called Adamnan warned that he had a dream in which he saw the monastery destroyed. The Coldingham monks behaved themselves for a while after Adamnan's warning.

Then they went back to their old ways and the monastery was destroyed by fire in AD 679. Bede said the fire was God's punishment.

So, be warned!

In 734 Bede himself was complaining in a letter to the Bishop of York:

Your Grace,

As you are aware, a monk vows to lead a single life, without the company of women. I was disgusted to note that monks in one of your monasteries were not only married – they were living in the monastery with their wives and children!

Bede also whinged about priests. They were guilty of 'laughter, jokes, stories, feasting and drunkenness'. Bede would not be someone you'd want to invite to your school Christmas party, then.

Even a strict monastery like Bede's own Monkwearmouth had problems with boys who preferred playing to praying. Just fifty years after Bede's death a monk was complaining that boys at Monkwearmouth monastery were having a wild time hunting foxes and hares! Monk Alcuin wrote:

How wicked to leave the service of Christ for a fox hunt

Misery for monks

Some monasteries could be very strict in their discipline. Boys were beaten with canes or whips for any misbehaviour. (Like dripping hot candle-wax on to an old monk's bald patch!)

But growing up didn't save you! Any monk could be punished by:

- beatings
- being locked in a cell alone
- being fed only bread and water.

Monks who did something really wicked (like eating meat on a Friday) would be thrown out of the monastery.

Just like schools until the 1960s really.

Nasty for nuns

Women had their own monasteries, called convents, but often shared mixed monasteries with monks. It's no surprise that the nuns got all the cooking and cleaning, sewing and serving jobs, is it?

Girls who became nuns must have liked larking about the way girls do today because there were rules to stop them. So, in the bedrooms, the nuns slept in rows – and the young nuns had old nuns sleeping between them to stop any joking, bullying or pillow fights (as girls tend to do, so they tell me).

But the naughtiest nun crime was 'vanity' – admiring your own good looks and sitting around in front of mirrors all day.

The nuns brought in one strict rule:

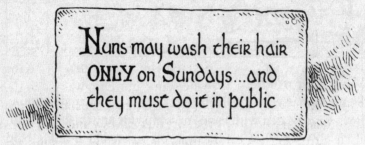

Nuns may wash their hair ONLY on Sundays...and they must do it in public

How would you like *that* rule, girls?

Suffering saints

Monks spent much of their time writing out the lives of saints. The tales of these weird and wonderful men and women were as exciting as a *Horrible Histories* book – but as believable as Enid Blyton!

Still, a saint's day was a good excuse for a holiday, so here are some excuses for a few days off from school. Just tell teacher you're a Saxon! You make up your own mind as to how true some of the curious cases on the calendar are.

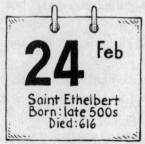

24 **Feb**

Saint Ethelbert
Born: late 500s
Died: 616

In 597 all England was a pagan country. Then Saint Augustine landed in King Ethelbert's kingdom and Eth said, 'I shall not harm you,' which was pretty nice, for a Saxon. King Eth not only made St Gus welcome but had himself and most of his people converted to Christianity.

48

This was the first ever Christian kingdom in England, so Eth became a saint. He didn't have to starve or suffer some other horrible death! Even you could be a saint if it's that easy!

Celebrate by going up to a passing monk and saying, 'I will not harm you!'

19 May

Saint Dunstan
Born: 909
Died: 988

A top saint in late Saxon Britain. Started in the court of King Athelstan – but Dun was given the boot for being a magician (no, not the sort that waves wands and pulls rabbits out of hats). Yet Dun *did* seem to have magic powers because he saw the murder of King Edmund before it happened (but never got to warn dead Ed). And an angel appeared on the road to tell Dun that King Eadred was dying – the shock of meeting the angel actually killed Dun's horse!

Dun set up a monastery and a school and for that he became a saint. Would you make your school teacher a saint?

Celebrate by waving a magic wand and making your school disappear!

23 June

Saint Etheldreda
Born: early 600s
Died: late 600s

A Saxon princess who wanted to become a nun but had to get married. Happily her husband died … well, not so happily for him. But, would you believe it, she had to take a second husband. She was such a miserable wife he eventually divorced her and let her get on with her nunning. She gave up fine clothes and wore rough wool, only washed with cold water and caught the plague. Like most plague victims she had a dirty great lump on her neck. She said, 'This is God's punishment because I once wore a rich necklace there! Cccct!' and she died. When her coffin was opened 16 years after her death the lump on her neck was … gone! She became the saint of people with sore throats.

Celebrate by washing your wool shirt in cold water, throwing away your necklaces and marrying twice.

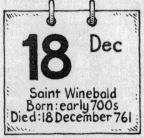

18 Dec

Saint Winebald
Born: early 700s
Died: 18 December 761

Saxon Winebald went off to Rome with his dad and his brother Willibald. (Note: I did not make up these silly names. Blame their dad, Saint Richard the Saxon.) Anyway, he set up a monastery in Germany and built a nunnery next door for his sister Walburga to run. Winebald was a poorly old man but he battled on bravely through great pain to do this Christian work. At least he got to be a saint when he died.

Celebrate by taking an aspirin – and writing a letter to your parents: 'Dear parents, thanks for not calling me Walburga, Winebald or Willibald!'

Saxon skills

Saxons had to have lots of skills to make the things they needed. Take something simple like making leather. Would you have the stomach for this lousy job?

Lousy leather

Animal skin rots and lets in water unless it is 'tanned' to turn it into leather. That's something even cave people knew and they made the animal skins into leather by pounding them with animal fat and brains! If they turned the leather into wooden-soled shoes they'd have real clever clogs! (Oh, never mind.)

Anyway, Lloyds Bank in York is on the site of a Saxon leather-making shop – a 'tannery'. Archaeologists dug there and found some interesting – but disgusting – facts about Saxon leather ...

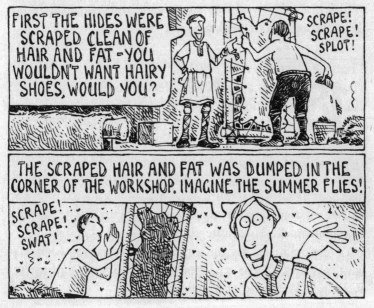

FIRST THE HIDES WERE SCRAPED CLEAN OF HAIR AND FAT - YOU WOULDN'T WANT HAIRY SHOES, WOULD YOU?

SCRAPE! SCRAPE! SPLOT!

THE SCRAPED HAIR AND FAT WAS DUMPED IN THE CORNER OF THE WORKSHOP. IMAGINE THE SUMMER FLIES!

SCRAPE! SCRAPE! SWAT!

You can imagine a Saxon warrior running away from a battle with the Vikings and claiming it was his shoes that ran away ... 'cos they were chicken!

Monk-y business

Making books was even messier than making leather. Monks used to murder kids to make books! Nah! I mean young goats – kids. What did you think I meant? They also massacred lambs and cut up calves in their thousands.

When well-behaved monks weren't praying, working in the fields, praying, helping the poor and needy, praying, sleeping in an unheated room, praying, eating some foul mush ... or praying ... they wrote books. Because printing hadn't been invented, they mostly copied other books by hand – the Bible and lives of saints and other people's work. Some brilliant monks, like Bede, wrote new books, including the first history of the English people.

There was also a whole horrible industry of monks providing the writing materials, because a monk couldn't pop down to the local corner shop for a pencil and paper. They hadn't been invented either! No, a lot of lambs and calves had to die to make those books.

NOTE: Vegetarians should skip this section.

Monks wrote on sheets of animal skin called 'vellum'. This is how you make vellum.

TRIM THE EDGES STRAIGHT AND KEEP THEM BETWEEN WOODEN BOARDS SO THEY DON'T CURL BACK UP INTO THE CUTE LITTLE SHAPE OF A CUTE LITTLE LAMB'S BELLY

The books from the 500s were all made on good quality skins. But by the end of the Dark Ages there were so many monks murdering so many lambs and calves and goats that they became a bit careless about the scraping and the vellum is sometimes as rough as a badger's bum.

Perfect pens and ideal ink

Next you needed a pen made from a stiff bird's feather, or quill. This was not quite as cruel as making the vellum because you didn't have to kill the birds to take their quills!

Take a seagull's or a goose's feather – it won't hurt much. (It's no more cruel than sneaking up behind a teacher and pulling a clump of their hair out with one sharp tug.) Wash the feather in hot water, then dry it. Trim off the feathery part with a sharp knife (careful!) to leave only the central shaft. Now you need to cut the end square. Finally cut away the back of the nib and make a slit half a centimetre up the shaft.

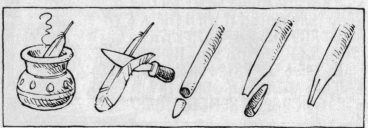

So now we've got the paper, or vellum, and pen. Of course being a big-brained *Horrible Histories* reader you'll have spotted what's missing. That's right ... ink!

Who has to suffer to make the ink? Intsy-winsy baby wasps, that's who ...

WASPS CHEW INTO THE BARK OF AN OAK AND LAY THEIR EGGS

OW!

THE TREE FORMS THIS LITTLE LUMP CALLED A GALL AROUND THE EGGS

OW!!

WE PULL OFF THE GALL AND CRUSH IT WITH THE WASP EGGS IN VINEGAR

OW!!!

WE ADD THE CHEMICAL COPPER-WATER TO GIVE THE COLOUR AND SOME GUM TO THICKEN IT

OW!!!!

Did you know … ?

One book that remains from the early 700s is called *The Lindisfarne Gospels*. It took the skin of at least 129 calves so it's not suitable for reading by vegetarians.

You are only able to read this *Horrible Histories* book because monks wrote down all that history. Thousands of creatures died so you could read this book!

I hope you feel ashamed of yourself!

Games you wouldn't want to play

Life could be cruel and so sports could be crueler. Don't try these at home …

Pony clubbing

What you need:
Two stallion horses
(bad tempered ones are best)
A square of fencing
A couple of sharp sticks

How to play:
Put the two stallions in the square together. They will start to fight. (If they're in a good mood then jab them with sticks to make them wild.)

I THINK THIS ONE'S WILD NOW

Urge the stallions to attack each other with teeth and hooves. The winner is the first stallion to flatten the other.
How to win:
Bet on the horse you think will win.

Bull-baiting

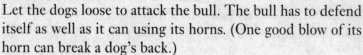

What you need:
A bull chained to a wooden stake
Dogs
How to play:
Let the dogs loose to attack the bull. The bull has to defend itself as well as it can using its horns. (One good blow of its horn can break a dog's back.)
How to win:
Bet on how many dogs the bull can kill.

Did you know … ?
Christian Saxons were expected to give up drinking in the weeks leading up to Easter. The writer Aelfric told of a man who broke this rule. He got very drunk, wandered out into the street where a bull was being baited and was gored to death by the bull. Aelfric said this was God's punishment on the drinker. But then God didn't punish the bull-baiters!

Terrible truths or foul fibs?

Truth is stranger than fiction, someone very clever and very boring once said. But you have to be able to tell the difference.

First take a passing parent (or priest) and sit them in a chair. (You may have to tie them there, so have a clothes-line handy.)

Say: 'You have to help me with my homework!' Then pester your parent (or perplex your priest) with this cunning cwiz and see if they can sort out the truth from the fibs.

1 The Saxons played bagpipes.

2 The Saxons dressed in nettles.

3 The Saxons built their houses out of pig poo.

4 Saxon shepherds were paid with cattle dung.

5 Saxon gold coins were often fakes because they didn't have a test for gold.

6 The Vikings raided Saxon towns when they knew they would be deserted.

7 The wheelbarrow was invented in Saxon times.

8 If someone wanted half a penny in Saxon times then they cut a penny coin in half.

Answers:

1 True … probably! They certainly had flutes and trumpets, harps and whistles, but some archaeologists believe they had bagpipes too.

AREEEEEEEAAAAEEEEEEEE EEEEEAAAEEEEEEEEE

OH HOW I WISH THE ARCHAEOLOGISTS WERE WRONG

2 True. The stems of the nettles were crushed and dried. They could then be woven into a cloth to make clothes. Imagine wearing nettle knickers!

3 True. First they planted posts in the ground, then wove branches between the posts. But there were lots of gaps. The walls had to be plastered with mud, though pig droppings could be slapped on and would dry to make a nice hard wall. Don't you wonder how they trained the pigs to poo on the walls? Hey! You don't suppose the Saxons just went around picking the stuff up in their bare hands, do you?

HOUSEBUILDERS AND DIY

SAXONS

NEW

QUICK SET PIG POO

500g

4 True. The shepherd was given 12 days' supply of cattle droppings as a special Christmas treat. He could spread it over his fields as fertilizer. Shepherds were

59

also allowed to keep one lamb and one fleece each year in payment. Maybe you'd like to revive this old Saxon custom and give a few buckets of manure to your best friend on Christmas Day? Then again, you may prefer to give it to your worst enemy.

5 False. The Saxons weren't great scientists but they did know how to test for gold. The king had a water butt with a fixed level of water in it. He took a certain weight of metal. If it was gold the water rose to just below the brim. If some cheap metal had been mixed in then the water overflowed. Water clever lot they were!

6 False. The Vikings raided on holy days when they knew the towns would be full of pilgrims, women and children going to church. These unarmed people would be snatched and sold as slaves as far away as north Africa. The Saxons weren't a lot better – the church objected to *Christians* like themselves being sold as slaves; they didn't object to other people being made slaves.

7 True. BUT … not by the Saxons. It was invented by the Chinese and won't be seen in Europe till the 1200s. The Saxons hadn't even invented buttons – they had to use brooches and cords.

8 True. Don't try cutting a pound coin in half if your local sweet shop wants 50p – it's now against the law.

Awful Offa, Alf and Ath

An Offa lot of wealth

In 757 King Aethelbald (who wasn't bald), king of the Mercians, died. He was a tough old goat who chased women – and often caught them! He was also very violent. Of course some people didn't like him and he got himself murdered by the men who were supposed to protect him – his bodyguards.

But where did they get the idea to murder their boss? The finger of suspicion points at King Offa who took the throne. Offa went on to rule Mercia in the middle of England – he was the meat in a sandwich of the Northumbrians (the Saxons in the north) and the Saxons of the south. He also had a lot of trouble with the wild Welsh. That's probably why he built a wide ditch and mound to keep them out of his kingdom.

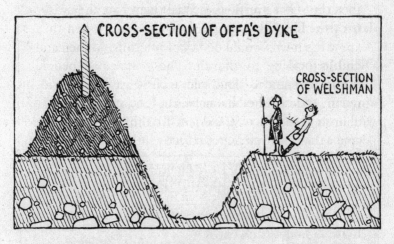

Offa also had trouble with the kings in the tribes he took over. They weren't all happy about paying 'tribute' to Offa. Every year they had to meet him and give him payment.

This could be …

- Money, gold brooches and precious metals.
- Cattle and horses, hawks and hounds (for hunting).
- Decorated swords with magical spells on them.
- A feather bed and fine linen bed sheets.

They also had to send men to fight for Offa and almost certainly had to send the men who dug his 150 mile ditch on the Welsh border.

In return Offa's army protected them – or at least didn't destroy them!

Offa his food

Offa also demanded 'food-rent'. He travelled around his kingdom and expected his nobles to feast and entertain him with lots of grub. How would you like the bill for feeding 150 people a day? Bet you hope and pray he doesn't stay a week!

Warning people Offa

One king who grew tired of paying Offa was Aethelberht of East Anglia. Old coins gives us a clue to what happened ...

THE MERCIAN COINS HAD THE NAME AND THE PICTURE OF OFFA ON THEM. BUT AROUND 790 NEW COINS APPEARED...

LOOK! A COIN WITH AETHELBERHT'S NAME AND HEAD ON

WHAT DOES THAT MEAN DAD?

IT MEANS AETHELBERHT IS A REBEL

WHAT'LL HAPPEN TO HIM, DAD?

OFFA WILL DEAL WITH HIM IF HE EVER FINDS OUT

WILL HE FIND OUT?

YES! 'COS I'M GOING TO TELL HIM, SON

THAT'S A BIT SNEAKY, DAD!

The murder of Aethelberht shocked many Mercians and their other Saxon neighbours – but it kept them in line.

Mercian misery

Offa died in 796 and his son died a few months later. The kings in East Anglia and Kent revolted against the miserable Mercian rule straight away – this was the chance they'd been waiting for.

The rebels of Kent were led by a monk-king Eadberht. He was captured but the merciful Mercians *didn't* execute him, the way Offa would have done.

YEAH! WE JUST CHOPPED HIS HANDS OFF AND GOUGED HIS EYES OUT

THANKS, GUYS!

But the days of Mercian mastery were numbered once their great king hopped Offa the twig. Offa had created the idea that England could be one kingdom with one king. Yet it *wasn't* the Mercians who went on to rule that kingdom – it was the West Saxons.

When Offa died in 796 there were four great Saxon kingdoms in England – his Mercia, Wessex (West Saxons), East Anglia and Northumbria. By 878 only the kingdom of Wessex had survived.

Tough luck Offa, after you went to all that boffa …

What went wrong? The Vikings, that's what.

Silver and geld

The Saxons had come as raiders. Once they'd conquered the Brits they settled down as farmers and forgot how to fight.

So along came the Vikings from Denmark as raiders; they conquered the Saxons and settled down as farmers. If the Saxons could hang on long enough the Vikings might just forget how to fight too!

King Alfred was the first to fight back. But he wasn't quite ready to go into battle. So, at first, he just paid the Vikings to leave him alone. This payment to the Danish Vikings has become known as 'Danegeld'.

As you'll read later, Ethelred the Unready has been called nasty names by historians because he paid fortunes in Saxon money to the Vikings so they'd go away. But those historians like to forget it was Alfred the 'Great' who did it first!

As a modern poet, Rudyard Kipling wrote, paying Danegeld was a pointless waste of money ...

> *And that is called paying the Dane-geld;*
> *But we've proved it again and again,*
> *That if once you have paid him the Dane-geld*
> *You never get rid of the Dane.*

Did you know ... ?

Saxon coins were made by 'moneyers' in the king's mint. They had the pattern on a stamp and hit the blank discs of silver with the stamp. The seventy mints made as many as five million coins a year this way!

A moneyer could become rich by making each coin just a little bit smaller than he was supposed to and saving all the little scraps of silver to build up a million-scrap fortune. BUT ... Athelred's Code of Laws said ...

> If a moneyer is found guilty of making coins too small then the hand that committed the crime shall be cut off and fastened to the mint.

66

Would that make a good punishment for shop assistants who give short change today?

Alf and Ath fight back

When the Danegeld ran out the Vikings squidged the Wessex king, Alfred, and his few hundred followers on to the marshes at Athelney. Alf broke out and gave the Vikings such a battering they made peace – and their king even became a Christian. Alf christened the Viking leader (Guthrum) himself.

Alf has become an English hero because the history books said he was a great leader. Who had the history books written? Alf, of course.

Alf's grandson, Athelstan, took the throne twenty-five years after Alf died and he set about snatching back all of England from the Viking settlers. He conquered England from Northumbria down to the south coast. Then he set about making the wild Welsh obey him. What a great guy. But Athelstan is forgotten in history books. Why? Because he didn't have history books written about his great victories.

History can be very unfair. It can also be full of fibs.

Hot hero

Alf, for example, is famous for the story of burning the cakes. Alf was in disguise, hiding from the Vikings (they said) when he went to a poor cottage for shelter. As the monks of St Neotts wrote over 250 years after Alf the Great died ...

THE FOLLOWING STORY IS 110% TRUE AND NOT ONE WORD OF A LIE. CROSS MY HEART AND HOPE TO DIE! HONEST! TRUTHFULLY, SINCERELY. THIS IS A LIE-FREE ZONE!

One day a peasant woman, the wife of a cowherd, was making loaves. King Alfred was sitting by the fire, looking after his bow and arrows and other weapons.

The poor woman saw that the loaves she'd put over the fire were burning. She ran up and took them off and scolded the unbeatable king. 'Look there, man! Couldn't you see the loaves were burning? Why didn't you turn them over? I'm sure you'd be the first to eat them if they were nicely done!'

The miserable woman did not realize that this was King Alfred, who had fought so many wars against the pagans and won so many victories.

The story is almost certainly a lie. But it makes Alf look like a struggling soldier, driven to hiding in the hut of a poor woman and getting nagged. What a hero he must have been to rise from that to defeat the Vikings, you'd say. Alfred is remembered for lies like this.

Athelstan didn't have historians to lie for him so he's forgotten.

But enough of these half-baked jokes.

Woeful for women

Digging up Saxon graves gives us clues about the different jobs men and women did. For example, women's graves often contained sewing boxes, so they must have been responsible for the sewing in their household, and it was probably seen as an important job.

In Saxon poetry women had a hard life and suffered it without complaining. In the real world it probably wasn't all bad. For example, unlike in many periods in history, women could be landowners ... though the only land some women got was a six foot grave.

A grave problem

One early Saxon grave was uncovered in layers. Could *you* be an archaeologist and explain what was most likely to have happened?

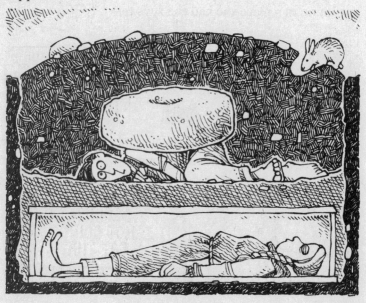

Explanation: The rich woman died, was put in her coffin and buried. The coffin was covered with a layer of soil and the second woman was thrown in – alive. The stone was placed on top of her to keep her there while the soil was piled on top to bury her alive.

It's harder to explain 'Why?' The second woman was possibly a slave sent to serve the rich woman in the afterlife. As if it wasn't bad enough being a slave in *this* life!

The key to success

In some women's graves there are sets of keys. This was a sign that women looked after the family's possessions and ran the house. (It makes you wonder how they got back in the house after the funeral when the keys were six foot under!)

Saxon law said that if stolen money was found in her house, the woman of the house was not to blame – unless it was found in a place she had the keys to.

And if a stolen animal was found in her house then the woman would not be blamed, so long as she swore not to eat the meat!

71

Wife weplacement

Divorce was rare … but there was another way to take a second wife while the first one was still alive. If your wife was carried away by an enemy you must try to buy her back. But, if you can't afford to pay for her then you can take a new wife instead!

If a man was fed up with his first wife (and that has been known to happen) then he must have been tempted to go around making enemies. But there must have been a bit of girl-power in Saxon times. If a man was captured by an enemy then a wife could take a new husband the same way.

YOO-HOO! MR VI-KING! MY HUSBAND'S OVER THERE!

Mystic mugs

Crystal balls have been found in some Saxon graves – usually the graves of women. These wise women used them to tell the future and were called 'heahrune'.

But if a wise woman used her mystic powers to work wicked magic then she was called a 'haegtessan' … a witch. And some still use the word 'hag' to insult a woman. (But *you* would never, ever, ever use such words about your teacher, would you?)

The witches

If you were a Saxon you probably believed that demons in the dark had the power to make a deal with you! They would give you magical powers on Earth … but as soon as you died then the Devil himself would come and take you away. If you agreed to that deal then you became a witch.

There is a story of a Saxon woman in the 800s who made such a deal with the Devil. Her story was turned into a poem a thousand years later by the Poet Laureate, Robert Southey (1774-1843)[1]. When the Devil sent his messenger raven, the old woman knew her time was up …

The Devil's Due

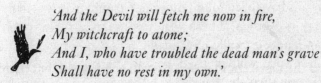

The raven croaked as she sat at her meal,
And the old woman knew what he said.
And she grew pale at the raven's tale,
And sickened and went to bed.

'I've anointed myself with infant's fat.
The devils have been my slaves.
From sleeping babes I have sucked the breath,
I have called the dead from their graves.

'And the Devil will fetch me now in fire,
My witchcraft to atone;
And I, who have troubled the dead man's grave
Shall have no rest in my own.'

1. The 'Poet Laureate' is supposed to be Britain's best living poet of the time. He (it's always been a 'he') is paid by the king or queen to write royal poems from time to time. Sadly being made 'Poet Laureate' doesn't mean you're always a very good poet.

They blest the old woman's winding sheet
With rites and prayers that were due.
With holy water they sprinkled her shroud,
And they sprinkled her coffin too.

And in he came with eyes of flame –
The Devil to fetch the dead.
And all the church in his presence glowed
Like a fiery furnace red.

He laid his hands on the iron chains;
And like flax they mouldered asunder.
And the coffin lid which was barred so firm
He burst with his voice of thunder.

And he called the old woman of Berkeley to rise
And come with her master away.
A cold sweat started on that cold corpse,
And the voice she was forced to obey.

The devil he flung her on a horse,
And he leapt up before.
And away like the lightning's speed she went;
And she was seen no more.

You'll notice the 'witch' was an old woman. The Saxons believed the Devil could possess a man *or* a woman, but there were many old tales such as this where women were the main suspects. Old women could not defend themselves so it was easy to accuse them of witchcraft and punish them.

Being a Saxon woman had its problems.

Did you know … ?

A Saxon man could suffer an 'illness' from 'a woman's chatter'! It had its own cure like many other illnesses.

Men's Own Saxon Weekly

73

CUT THE CACKLE

Have you ever had a hard day on the farm only to come home to an earful of woman's talk? Are you needlessly nagged? Does gossip make you gag? In short, do you suffer from a woman's chatter?

Then old Doctor Bald's leechbook has the answer!

Just take a radish – yes one of those hot, red veggies – and eat it before you go to bed. But beware, boys – eat nothing else!

 Next morning the woman may still be wittering but you'll find it no longer bothers you!

Of course men today just love listening to women talk!

The cruel cave

The trouble with being a woman in Saxon times was that the world was run by men. Your life was decided by your father while you were a child, and your husband when you were married. That may have been fine for many women. But if a husband had problems then his wife would suffer too … maybe even worse!

There is an old Saxon poem called 'The Wife's Lament' preserved in *The Exeter Book* that's kept now in Exeter Cathedral. It's about a woman who came from overseas to marry a man. The man didn't tell her that he was mixed up in a feud and he soon had to escape to save his life. She was left behind, in a strange land, and had to live hidden in a cave beneath an oak tree.

The Saxon poets would go to feasts and sing her sad story ...

I've never known such misery since I became his wife,
Abandoned by a husband who sailed off to save his life.

A victim of a vicious feud, he had to leave me here,
And hide me deep within these woods where I must live in fear.

I live beneath an ancient oak, within a deep earth cave,
Alive, and yet it seems to me, I'm living in my grave.

Each dawn I rise and leave the cave to walk through twisted trees,
And moan when I remember how my lord is overseas.

Sad grief is all there is for those who have to live apart.
No friends, no parents and no love. Alone with aching heart.

It's enough to put you off your feast, isn't it?

I suppose it's no worse than watching some miserable television programme while you're chewing your chips or slurping your soup.

We'll have none of that ear
A married woman in late Saxon times could *not* go off with another man. If she did, the church law said ...

...her husband shall take all her property and she is to lose her nose and ears.

Married men didn't suffer that punishment if they went off with another woman. This law didn't last long and was changed in 1035.

What would the world be like if we had that law today? Who nose?

Saxon scoffers

No baked beans, no chocolate, no chips. Would you really like to have lived in those days? Like most other ages in horrible history a lot might depend on whether you were a rich noble or a pathetic peasant. For example …

Gut grub

Take 10 jars of honey, 300 loaves of bread, 42 casks of ale, 2 oxen, 10 geese, 20 hens, 10 cheeses, 1 barrel of butter, 5 salmon and 100 eels. What have you got?

1 The food supply for one peasant family for one year?
2 The food supply for one rich farmer for one year?
3 The food eaten by a Saxon king and his friends in one *night*?

The last one, of course. There's no mention of how many indigestion tablets they needed next day.

Putrid pottage

Peasant food was plain and boring. The bread was coarse with grit from the grinding stones. Saxon skeletons found by archaeologists have teeth worn away by chewing bread like sandpaper.

Monasteries grew their own food but it could be pretty boring stuff. A vegetable stew (called 'pottage') would have been a common meal. If you'd like to know how the monks ate then try this recipe …

Monks' Mush (or Nuns' Nosh)

Here's a tasty treat for you starving sisters and brothers. Eat this three times a day to grow healthy and fit. You may not live to thirty with a potty pottage diet − but life will be so miserable you'll be happy to die!

You need:
1 leek
1 onion
half cup of peas
half cup of lentils
half litre of water
pinch of parsley
pinch of sage
salt

Cooking:
Peel and chop the onion and the leek.
Boil the water and add the parsley, sage and salt.
Add the onion, leek, peas and lentils.
Cover and boil slowly for half an hour.
Serve with thick chunks of bread.

You may enjoy this recipe. But if you try eating it three times a day, seven days a week for most of your life, you may just get a teeny-weeny bit bored with it.

Run, rabbit, run!

St Benedict made the rules that monks lived by. One rule said they should not eat flesh. But monks took this to mean they should not eat four-legged animals. They ate fish and birds – and they even ate beavers because (they said) beavers live in water, so they're fish! But, strangest of all, the Normans brought rabbits to Britain when they conquered it in 1066, and monks decided it was all right to eat them!

Test your teacher on taste

Ask your teacher these questions about Saxon food. See if they can score ten out of ten! Which of these foods did Saxons eat?

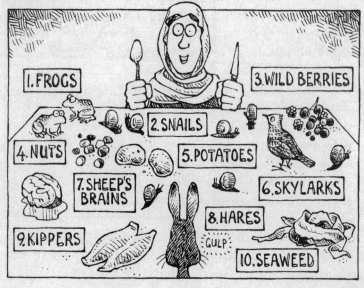

1. FROGS
2. SNAILS
3. WILD BERRIES
4. NUTS
5. POTATOES
6. SKYLARKS
7. SHEEP'S BRAINS
8. HARES
9. KIPPERS
10. SEAWEED

Hunger horrors

Some of the things Saxons ate may seem disgusting to you – you don't see many sheep brains on the school dinner menu, do you? But there was something worse than eating seaweed sandwiches, and that was eating nothing at all.

Food didn't keep for very long – no fridges in Saxon houses. You grew food in summer and ate it over the winter. But if you failed to grow the food in the summer then you starved over winter.

What would stop you growing food in summer? Well …

- Bad weather, heavy rain, floods or storms destroying your wheat.
- Viking invaders burning your fields and stealing your cattle.
- Plagues killing off farm workers and animal plagues destroying your flocks.

What could you do?

- Jump off a cliff.
- Eat your neighbours.
- Sell your children.
- Put your head in your lord's hands.
- Eat a tree.

Do they sound daft? Well they're horribly historically true, as the chronicles of the time tell …

OUR FAMINE FAVOURITES

Crops failed? Got a rumbling tum? Then try these top tips from the *Anglo-Saxon Chronicle* and see how you can cure those hunger pains!

1 Fall in line

In Sussex last year forty villagers cured their hunger for good. They went to the edge of a cliff, joined hands and jumped over. The ones who weren't crushed on the rocks were drowned in the sea. Fast food for fish!

2 Funeral food

It's been reported that when villagers died in a famine area they were not buried by their families (as that would be a waste of good meat). Instead they were cooked and eaten. Human hotpot saves lives.

3 Slave away

The Saxon law says: 'A father may sell a son if that child is under seven years old and if he needs to do so.' Selling children earns you money ... plus you save because you don't have to feed them! No kids is good kids – no kidding!

4 Good Lord!

It is a lord of the manor's duty to protect his people. If the worst comes to the worst visit your local lord, kneel in front of him and place your head in his hands. You then become his slave and work for him – but at least he'll feed you.

5 Tree-mendous!

When all else fails you can eat everything in sight. It's been reported that Saxon survivors ground up anything from acorns to tree-bark, nettles and wild grass to fill out the flour. Your bark can be good for your bite!

Muttering monks

It's nice to sit down at a table, eat good food and gossip with a friend. But monks were supposed to be silent while they ate their food. That's not just boring … it can also be a real nuisance. What about if you need something desperately? Don't worry – the monks had their own system of signs.

Try eating school dinners in silence (your teachers will like this historical game!) and use the monk system instead of words. Here are four to get you started.

Monastery messages

1. 'Pass the salt' – place three fingers together and shake them as if salting something

2. 'Pass the pepper' – knock two fingers together

3. 'Pour me some wine' – put thumb and forefinger together as if turning on the tap of a cask

4. 'Pass the butter' – stroke three fingers of one hand over the palm of the other hand

There are an amazing 127 different signs in the monks' guidebook that you'd have to learn. Once you've mastered the four above then make up your own … but I don't want to see the one you make up for 'I think I'll go for a pee'.

Horrible historical joke
This witty riddle was written by a monk …

QUESTION: WHAT MAKES BITTER THINGS SWEET?
ANSWER: HUNGER

It's not a very good joke, but it's survived 1200 years, which is more than you will, so don't sneer at it!

Did you know … ?

November was known as 'Blood Month'. That month was when the Saxons slaughtered cattle because (a) they wanted to eat them over the winter months, and (b) they couldn't feed many of the beasts when there was no fresh grass. So it was bye-bye to your old friend Daisy the cow and hello to scrumptious steaks. Could you eat your old friend?

Sooty bacon
Saxon houses had no chimneys – the smoke just drifted upwards and out through a hole in the roof. When a pig was killed for food it was hung from the roof and the smoke 'cured' it; that is, it stopped it going bad. So a pig killed in autumn could still be eaten in spring.

And people today still enjoy the taste of smoked bacon. But modern smoky bacon is probably not as tasty as Saxon bacon which would have bits of soot from below, not to mention insects dropping down from the roof. Nothing nicer than a sprinkling of spider to add to your breakfast bacon!

The Tudors brought tobacco to Britain so maybe they invented the horrible historical joke ...

Bee brave and bee have!

There was no sugar in Saxon England. The only sweetener was honey, so a family celebrated when bees set up a hive in their roof.

There was one sure way of persuading bees to come to your home. When a swarm flies past you, grab a handful of gravel and throw it over them, crying the spell:

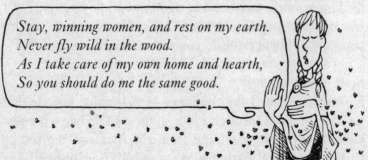

Stay, winning women, and rest on my earth.
Never fly wild in the wood.
As I take care of my own home and hearth,
So you should do me the same good.

Of course it may be dangerous to throw gravel at a swarm of bees. So get the nearest teacher to do it for you while you go inside and shut the doors and windows.

Curious cures

Luckily some marvellous medicine books have survived from the Saxon age. Books like *Bald's Leechbook* (Bald was the owner of the book) written in the late 800s. Some of the magical charms go back to Saxon days before they invaded England and are probably the oldest pieces of German writing we have.

Curl curing

The Saxons had their own treatments for baldness. You can't buy it at Boots, but you may like to offer a bald bloke you know this cure …

HORRIBLE HISTORIES® HAIR RESTORER

Is your Dad (or your history teacher) a slaphead? Is there more hair on a hen's egg than his skull's skin?

Then try Horrible Histories hair restorer!

Yes, this is simply made by burning bees and rubbing the ash into the shining scalp.

This wonder cure is absolutely free – and you get your money back if it doesn't work! You'll be your parent's pet for ever more!

Helping your hair gives me a real buzz!

You're a honey!

Or you could buy a wig.

Cute cures

Pagan and Christian ideas were mixed up when Saxons tried to cure sicknesses. Could you cure these six Saxons' sicknesses? (Cure it! You couldn't even say it!)

1.	2.	3.	4.	5.	6.
For a toothache	For a swelling on the eyelid	For a snake bite	For madness	For a sick horse	For a sick girl

a.

Take the skin of a dolphin, make it into a whip and beat yourself with it

b.

Boil a holly leaf, lay it on a saucer of water, raise to the mouth and yawn

c.

Cut the sign of the cross in the forehead, back and limbs, pierce the left ear, then beat with a stick

d.

Cut a vein and let out some blood. This must be done at night

e.

Take a knife and cut out the affected part

f.

Take a piece of wood from a tree grown in Heaven and press it to the wound

88

Answers:

1b) You will find (a Saxon medical book promises) that 'the evil tooth-worms will tumble from the mouth'. Yeuch! Think I'd prefer the toothache!

2e) A Saxon book says that a youth survived a knife through the eyelid. Even kings and queens suffered a bit of butchery. Queen Etheldrida had a swelling on her jaw and her doctor 'opened the swelling to let out the poisonous matter in it'. She'd have cried 'Ouch' but it's difficult crying anything with a knife in your jaw!

3f) You might well ask, 'How do you get wood from a tree grown in Heaven?' Well that's a stupid question, if I may say so. Just let the snakebite kill you, go to Heaven and get the wood to cure you. Simple!

SORRY. NOT STOPPING. JUST POPPED UP FOR A BIT OF TIMBER

4a) You may not be mad after the whipping – but the skinless dolphin will be absolutely furious.

5c) This treatment will make your horse a little cross – or six little crosses, to be accurate. You may find that your local vet does not use this old Saxon cure.

6d) A Saxon bishop warned doctors, 'Do not do this on the fourth day of a new moon!' What sort of clock did he use to measure the timing of the moon? A lunar-tick, of course!

Don't try these cures at home because you need the right magical spells to recite with the cure. When the Saxons became Christian the magical spells became Christian prayers – they would sing 'Misere me deus'[1] three times and recite the Lord's Prayer nine times.

Some other cures you probably shouldn't try …

1 Poisonous spider bite Make three cuts into the flesh near the bite. Let the blood run into a hazel-wood spoon. Throw the spoon *and* blood over the road. Messy!

2 Dog bite Burn the jaw of a pig to ashes. Sprinkle the ashes on to the wound. Mind the pig jaw doesn't bite you too!

3 Bleeding wound To stop the bleeding take the soot from a pot, rub it into a powder and sprinkle it on the wound. If that doesn't work then take fresh horse droppings, bake them dry and rub them into a powder – put the powder on to a thick linen cloth and bind it on to the wound overnight. Yeuch! Better to bleed!

4 Thick hair To thin your hair, burn a swallow to ashes and rub the ashes into the scalp. To completely stop hair growing then rub ant eggs into the scalp. What a yolk!

1. It means 'God have mercy on me'. You can try singing that instead and just hope that God speaks English!

5 Headache Take swallow-chicks and cut them open. Look for little stones in their stomachs, sew them into a bag and place on the head. This is also a cure for people plagued by goblins.

EEK!

OH NO! HE'S GOT SWALLOW-CHICK-STOMACH-STONES ON HIS HEAD!

Cuthbert's cure

If you are ill it helps to be a saint. When St Cuthbert had a swollen knee he was advised to cook wheat flour with milk and put the hot mixture on his knee. Who told him this? His doctor? No. An angel on a horse! (Why did the angel need a horse? Weren't his wings working? And if the angel is God's messenger, then why didn't God just cure the knee without all that gooey flour? Or why did God allow Cuthbert's knee to swell in the first place? Sometimes God can be a funny woman.)

Health horrors

The good news is Saxon adults were quite tall and strong. History lessons often say that people in the past were much smaller and weedier than we are today. That may have been true for the children of Queen Victoria's smoky slums. It wasn't true of the Saxons. (Archaeologists have measured the Saxon bones in graves and proved this. Nice job, eh?)

The bad news is only half the Saxons lived to see their 25th birthday.

More bad news is that there were a lot of diseases that couldn't be cured and were quite nasty.

Four foul health horrors that Saxons lived and died with were ...

1 Fleas Monks had four or five baths every year – outside the monasteries people probably had fewer – so fleas flew happily through clothes, scoffed on your skin and belched after a bellyful of your blood. One wacky cure was to take the flea-infested clothes and lock them in an air-tight box. They must have thought the fleas would starve or suffocate!

2 Lice These stubborn little friends lay their eggs in your hair and cling like a rottweiler to a burglar's bum. The Saxons used combs with very close teeth, dragged them through the hair and hoped to pull out the eggs and the lice – not to mention lumps of hair! St Cuthbert was buried with a comb made from an elephant's tusk – he must have had jumbo-sized lice!

3 Ergot Old grain went mouldy with a fungus called ergot. If you made the grain into flour and ate the fungus you got ergotism ... very nasty. If you are lucky you feel anxious, and dizzy, get noises in your ears, feel your arms and legs are on fire and can't stop them twitching. You dance out of control … but could recover. If you were unlucky you got the feeling of ants running round in your burning feet and fingers, which then turned red, then black, then dropped off. If you were really unlucky your ears and nose dropped off and you died. (But ergot was worse in France in the Dark Ages than in England, where victims usually recovered.)

4 Worms No, not the sort of squiggly, fat things you see in the ground. These were the ones that lived inside your body. The whipworm was harmless and stayed in your gut, but the monstrous maw-worm could grow to 30 centimetres and infest your liver or lungs. It could move through your body and pop out anywhere – including the corner of your eye! Yeuch!

Did you know …?
The Saxons had no idea of how diseases are spread by germs. If food fell on the floor amongst the dog droppings they'd just wipe it (to take away the taste) and make a sign of the cross (to take away any evil spirits that were hanging round there) … and then pop it into their mouth. Scrummy!

Ethelred the Ready for Beddy

Kwick king kwiz

King Ethelred II was given the name Ethelred 'the Unready'. How have teachers explained this nickname?

HE WAS UNREADY BECAUSE HE WAS NEVER READY WHEN THE VIKINGS INVADED

ETHELRED COULDN'T READ – HE WAS UN-READ, AS THEY SAY

THE SAXON WORD 'RAED' MEANS ADVICE. ETHELRED REFUSED TO TAKE ADVICE, SO HE WAS 'UN-RAEDY'

'RAED' MEANS ADVICE – BUT HE WAS 'UN-RAED' BECAUSE HE WAS GIVEN BAD ADVICE

TAFF NLY

Answer: At some time or another ALL of these different explanations have been given. The nickname was first written down two hundred years after his death but it could have been used during his lifetime. It was probably meant as a joke – Ethelred was both badly advised (un-raed) AND not ready for the Viking invasions.

And that's not the only unkind thing historians have said about Eth the pathetic ...

Unready, steady, go

Poor old Ethelred the Unready came to the throne in 978 and ruled until 1013. He has been remembered for a thousand years as one of the world's worst monarchs – and, as most monarchs have been pretty bad, that means Eth must have been totally useless!

Eth has been blamed for letting the Vikings return and rob the English till their purses and bellies were as empty as a traffic warden's heart. How did Eth get a thousand years of blame?

A hundred years after his death a monk, William of Malmesbury, wrote ...

> *The king was always ready for sleep and it was what he did best. He put off great matters like stopping the Danish Vikings and yawned. If he ever raised the strength to get up on one elbow then he fell back again, either because he couldn't be bothered or because he was driven back by bad luck.*

Of course Will of Malmesbury didn't mean Eth really spent all his time in bed. He just meant he was as dozy as someone who did. Yet Eth spent 38 years on the throne – so he must have been doing something right! And he didn't have a lot going for him:

- Bad-tempered, violent King Edward was murdered so his half-brother Ethelred could become king – church leaders made evil Edward a saint.
- Edward was murdered while he was visiting Ethelred – churchmen said killing the king brought a curse on Eth, even if he wasn't to blame for it.

- Eth was just ten years old when he took the throne – would you rule a country at that age?
- 'A cloud as red as blood' was seen after Eth was crowned – it appeared at midnight and vanished at dawn – it was a sign that God was angry.

Byrhtnoth the brave (but batty)

Eth wasn't the only one to blame for the Viking success. Byrhtnoth was an old but brave Saxon warrior. The Vikings landed on the little island of Northey in the River Blackwater near Maldon, Essex. Byrhtnoth's army faced them from the bank of the river, across the shallow water, and their fate was recorded in the heroic poem, 'The Battle of Maldon'.

First the Vikings demanded payment …

Bold Byrhtnoth replied …

Tough talk!

The island was joined to the shore by a strip of mud at low tide. As the Vikings tried to cross Byrhtnoth's men cut them down.

The Vikings said …

Byrhtnoth! We cannot fight like this. Let my men cross to the shore and give you a real battle!

What a joke! A wise old warrior would say, 'No!' In fact only a bird-brained booby would say, 'Yes.'

Byrhtnoth said, 'Yes.'

Byrhtnoth was a brave and heroic man. He was soon a brave and heroic corpse as the Vikings cut him and his men to pieces.

But at least he *tried* to fight back. King Ethelred simply said …

PAY THEM!

Gruesome at Greenwich

Ethelred had a fair idea of what might happen if he didn't pay the Vikings. Look at what happened to Archbishop Aelfheah!

If one of the serving women at a Viking stronghold could have written, this is how she may have described the grisly scene …

Greenwich
Near London
20 April 1012

Dear Mum,

I am sending you a few pieces of silver. I pinched them from the Danish Vikings here. Don't worry, they won't miss them — and anyway, they owe me the money after the way they've made me work! 'I'm not a slave!' I told them. At least I would have told them but I was a bit scared they'd make me one!

Anyway, last week they started collecting that tribute Ethelred and us Saxons have to pay. 48,000 pounds in silver! Agnes, who speaks a bit of Viking, says they were boasting that it would be about twelve million silver coins!

But last night they turned really

nasty. They robbed a trade ship on the river Thames and pinched barrels and barrels of French wine. Of course, being Vikings, they had to drink it all in one feast, didn't they? I was run off my feet keeping their goblets topped up. They poured it into their hairy faces as fast as I could pour it into the cups!

And a drunk Viking is a vile Viking, I can tell you. For a bit of sport they dragged the old Archbishop of Canterbury, Aelfheah, into the hall. He's been their prisoner for seven months. They started shouting at him, 'How much are you going to pay to set yourself free, you snotty Saxon?' (At least that's what Agnes said they said.)

The old arch-bish was so calm! He just said, 'Nothing. And I will not allow the king or my church to pay you anything! The poor should not have to pay taxes to set me free.'

Well, that drove the Vikings mad as a nest of vipers. One of the Viking warriors took his sword out and raised it over the old bloke's head. 'No silver, no Saxon!' he cried.

'Wait!' the Viking leader roared. 'You cannot spill the blood of a holy man. We'll be cursed!'

So the Viking warrior looked crafty and grinned a black-and-yellow-toothed grin. He picked up an ox bone from the feast and threw it at the old arch-bish. It cracked the old guy right on the conk and he fell. 'See! No blood!' the warrior laughed.

That gave them all the idea for a bit of sport! Every Viking picked up a bone and pelted the old man – some of them even threw ox heads at him that had been picked clean. The bish took it bravely for a while – then he fell. Only one brave Viking tried to stop them but they ignored him.

At last their leader walked up to the half-dead arch-bish. Aelfheah had converted him to Christianity just the day before so I expected him to help the bish! Huh! No chance. He simply smacked him with the blunt side of his axe to finish him off.

Then they went back to their drinking till they drank themselves senseless. When they were all snoring we had to drag the old man out of the feasting hall and me and Agnes took him to the local church.

I am absolutely shattered. Working all night, dragging bodies all morning. I tell you, Mum. If you see those Vikings heading for your house then run. And pray they don't find the bones our dog buried in the garden. Your loving daughter, Hilda

Aelfheah's death was remembered and a church built on the spot where he died. It's still there in Greenwich today while his body was taken back to Canterbury.

He was made a Saxon saint ... and probably deserved it!

Eth's death, then Ed's dead

Here's a totally useless bit of information for you to impress your teacher with:

In 1013 Viking king Swein arrived. (Rearrange the letters to make 'Swine' … which the Saxons must have called him!) Eth ran away to Normandy so the Vikings couldn't kill him.

Swein died in 1014. The Vikings wanted their Cnut to rule. But the Saxons welcomed back Ethelred … so long as he promised to be a better ruler. Then in 1016 he died. A really mean Victorian historian sneered …

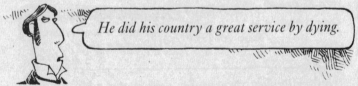

He did his country a great service by dying.

Eth's son, Edmund, gave Viking Cnut a few beatings in battle and they split the country between them, the way Alfred had – Danes in the north and east, Saxons in the south and west. It may have stayed like that but Ed did a really stupid thing – as daft as his dad Eth – he went and died! Cnut took over the whole country and Saxon rule was finished for 25 years.

How to be a Great king

Cnut may have been a Viking but a lot of historians think he was a 'good' king. He was named Cnut the Great. But we horrible historians know better. You don't get to be 'Great' without splattering blood around like water at a swimming gala.

Cnut was a Viking and he was a bad loser. He took Saxon hostages in East Anglia. When he was attacked by the Saxons he set sail into the English Channel. Cruel Cnut dropped the hostages off in Kent – but only after he'd dropped their hands and noses off into the sea.

Cnut was worried that Edmund's brothers would take over dead Ed's claim to the throne. He had Eadwig murdered.

To stop Edmund's step-bothers Edward and Alfred claiming dead Ed's throne he married their mother – if they fought him they'd have to fight their mum! Neither boy fancied that so they fled. Cnut was not bothered by the fact he already had a girlfriend and two sons (Swein and Harald) up in Northampton.

There were some English leaders that Cnut didn't trust. They had promised to obey him, but he wasn't sure. Just to be on the safe side he executed them. Earl Uhtred of Northumbria, for example, went to make peace with Cnut. Uhtred's own treacherous servant, Wighill, ran out from a hiding place and murdered him. It seems Cnut gave Wighill the order.

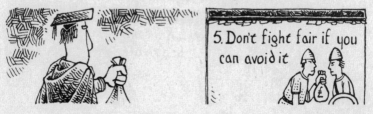

Cnut won a lot of battles. But he often cheated. When he attacked Norway in 1028 he sent large amounts of English money to princes so they would betray their king. Cnut conquered Norway with wallets for weapons.

6. Make promises you don't intend to keep

Cnut couldn't beat Edmund in the war for the English throne, until Ed was betrayed by Mercian lord Eadric. Cnut made peace with Edmund and they swore to be 'brothers' … and a few months later Edmund conveniently died. Surely Cnut the 'Great' wouldn't arrange to have a noble 'brother' bumped off!?! What do you think?

He was a tough nut (and a tough Cnut), but he was a 'Great' king – wasn't he?

Saxon crime and punishment

The Saxons certainly didn't mess about if you broke one of their laws.

King Edmund became an English saint – a good Christian who was captured by Viking bullies and chose to die horribly rather than give up his religion. You may be starting to feel sorry for Ed. DON'T!

Ed was not a kind and gentle king. Look at how he treated runaway slaves. (Slaves were known to the Saxons as 'thralls'.)

Grave for slaves

By the decree of King Edmund

WANTED

DEAD OR ALIVE

Thralls who have abandoned their masters and turned outlaw.
These men and women must be hunted and captured. Then an example must be made of those captured as follows:

Leaders – to be **hanged** in public
Other runaways – to be **flogged** three times, **scalped** and their little fingers **removed** before being returned to work

Painful punishment

In pagan Saxon times crimes were avenged by 'feuds' where people took the law into their own hands – you know, the sort of thing that still goes on in classrooms today …

The trouble is feuds could go on and on, maybe getting senseless and violent …

…and not even death stopped the feud …

So kings tried to replace revenge with payment ...

Even a human life could have a price on it – a 'weregild'. If a person were killed then the killer would have to make a weregild payment to the victim's family. The richer you were the higher your weregild was. A dead lord's family would get more than a dead peasant's family would from the killer.

Even bits of your body had a price on them!

What's your nose worth compared to your toes? Can you match the body bit to the money?

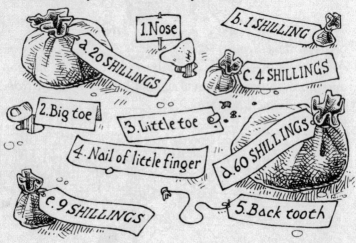

1. Nose
b. 1 SHILLING
a. 20 SHILLINGS
c. 4 SHILLINGS
2. Big toe
3. Little toe
4. Nail of little finger
d. 60 SHILLINGS
e. 9 SHILLINGS
5. Back tooth

Answers: 1d); 2a); 3e); 4b); 5c).

108

Whips and lips

Traitors, outlaws, witches, wizards and frequent thieves could all receive the death penalty. But the execution method varied from place to place, time to time and crime to crime. If you were caught, how would you like to go? Which of these Saxon punishments would you choose to suffer?

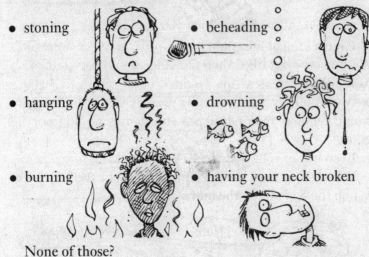

- stoning
- beheading
- hanging
- drowning
- burning
- having your neck broken

None of those?

All right. A merciful Saxon judge may teach you a lesson with a bit of mutilation – that is, he'd have bits cut off you. Which could you do without … ?

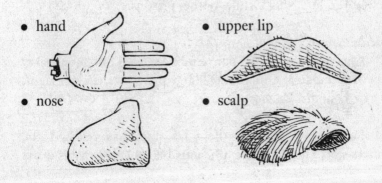

- hand
- upper lip
- nose
- scalp

- tongue
- ear
- eye
- foot

None of those either? Then you could be ...

- Branded with a hot iron

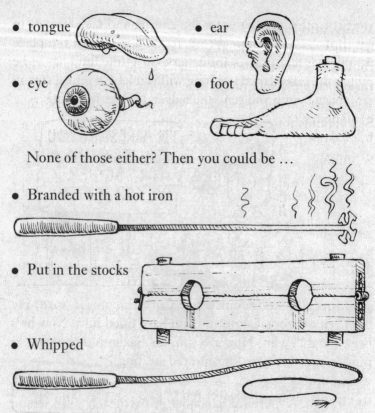

- Put in the stocks

- Whipped

You'd rather go to prison?

Sorry – there may be a cellar in the lord's manor house to hold you for a short while, but no prisons.

Judgement day

Saxons held their trials in assemblies called folk moots. Try being a judge at a folk moot. How many can you get right, your honour?

1 Sanctuary Geraint the goat thief has reached the monastery church where he claims 'sanctuary' – that is to say your law officers can't enter the church and take him off to jail. But if every criminal runs to the abbey then the place would be full of thieves and killers. So a time limit has to be put on the sanctuary. How long will you let a criminal stay in sanctuary before you send the lads in to drag him out?

a) 40 hours.
b) 40 days.
c) 40 years.

2 Thieves Some criminals like Cuthwine never learn. He has been caught stealing and you have fined him. Now he's been caught again. How are you, his Saxon judge, going to punish him this time for repeated stealing?

a) Cut off his hair.
b) Cut off his hand.
c) Cut off his head.

3 Child cruelty Some parents are accidentally cruel to their children because they try out 'cures' for illnesses without realizing the dangers. In the early 700s a law has been passed, as you know, your honour. It means you must sentence Brigit to five years of punishment if she does what to cure her daughter's fever?

a) Holds the child too close to the fire.

b) Ducks her in the village pond.

c) Puts her on the roof or puts her in the oven.

4 Foreigners Foreigners in Saxon England can't be trusted because they might be spies for an enemy. So a foreigner must stay on the main roads and tracks, and if he leaves the path he has to let everyone know by blowing a horn or shouting. Maelgwn has been arrested for breaking this law. What must you do to him, your honour?

a) Put him to death as a thief.

b) Send him back to his own country.

c) Fine him a penny for every step he took off the path.

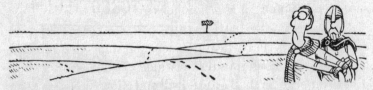

5 Fines There were no prisons in your local Saxon villages. Fines were easier to arrange. Which of these crimes must you punish with a fine, your honour?

a) Eating meat on a 'fast' or holy day.

b) Making a sacrifice to a pagan god.

c) Unlawful marriage.

IT'S MY FIRST FAST FEAST FINE!

6 Manslaughter Murder is not seen as a crime against the victim, but a crime against the victim's family. So, if a man is killed his family suffer because he is no longer there to earn a living for them. The family will demand his 'weregild' – his value in cash. But Benedict killed Alwin accidentally when a tree he was cutting fell on his neighbour. What must you order Benedict to do, your honour?

a) Pay the family the weregild money the same as for a murder.

b) Take the place of the victim in the family.

c) Kill himself.

7 Trials Edwin is suspected of stealing a pig. You ordered him to come to the village for a trial. (If Edwin doesn't turn up then he is 'Guilty'.) You have no police force to collect evidence – and no fingerprints to prove that a criminal was there. How can you check a suspect's story?

a) If he swears an oath on the Bible you must believe every word he says.

b) If he remains silent you must decide he is innocent.

c) If he swears an oath but stumbles over words (or stammers) you take it as a sign he is guilty.

8 Ordeals Egbert says he is innocent and wants to take a trial by 'ordeal' – a dangerous test in which God will protect him if he is innocent. What 'ordeal' will you allow Egbert to take?

a) He must grip a red–hot iron bar … and not be burned.

b) He must be tied up and thrown in the river … and float.

c) He must pull a stone from a pot of boiling water … and not be scalded.

9 Punishments Your court has found Theodoric guilty of witchcraft. You may choose to hang him. Which of these three other execution methods could you use in Saxon England, your honour?

a) Boiling.

b) Starving.

c) Guillotine.

113

10 Outlaws Cormac is a criminal who has run away from your punishment, then lived outside the law – he is declared an 'outlaw'. This means …

a) He doesn't have to pay taxes.

b) He is not allowed to go to church.

c) Anyone can kill him without having to stand trial for his murder.

Answers:

1b) Sanctuary lasted 40 days. But you only got 40 days if you handed over your weapons. If the criminal hadn't escaped in those 40 days he was taken to court and tried. Criminals could also claim sanctuary in a royal household! (They couldn't be throne out!) The trouble is someone has to sit outside the church for forty days to make sure he doesn't escape. Talk about crimewatch.

2b) A criminal could have his hand cut off, especially someone who stole from a church. Another common punishment was to 'brand' a criminal – burn a mark on his skin – so that everyone could see what he'd been up to and take extra care of their belongings when he was around.

A THIEF *AND* A POISONER?

WORSE! TEACHER'S PET!

3c) The writer of the law claimed that women put their daughters on the roof or in the oven to cure a fever! Do NOT let your mother read this book in case she gets some sad Saxon idea into her head and pops you in to bake.

4a) Very harsh, but in the days when very few people left their own village strangers were seen as dangerous. Even a great teacher and preacher like Bede never went further than a hundred miles north or south of his home monastery. Nowadays we're more trusting of strangers – even if they come from Clacton-on-Sea!

5a), b) and **c)** These were *all* fined.

6a) 'Blood money' had to be paid to the family of a victim, even if it was an accident.

7c) The accused could also call witnesses in his defence. Each witness would swear an oath that the accused was innocent. If enough witnesses took the oath *without a mistake* then that was also seen as a sign of innocence.

8 a), b) and **c)** *All* of these were Saxon tests of guilt. The hot iron bar must be carried one to three metres before being dropped. You can try this in class – you suspect Bertram Brown of pinching your pencil? See if he can carry a hot dog three metres without being burned!

9a) As well as boiling, burning was also a Saxon execution method.

10c) Outlaws did not have the protection of the law. Catch one and you could do whatever you liked with him – use him for target practice, get him to do your washing up or your homework or walk your pet rabbit. What would *you* use a captive outlaw for?

THE SCHOOL BULLY JUST HIT ME – HIT HER BACK!

Did you know … ?

Not all of the early Saxon judges had been just or honest. They did favours for friends and filled their pockets with fines. King Alfred the Great made the Saxon courts much fairer. He sorted out the cheating judges and replaced them with honest ones. What happened to the dishonest judges? Alfred had them hanged. They didn't do as much cheating after that.

Not-so-sweet sixteen

If you committed a crime you were punished, whatever your age … until King Athelstan came along. One case changed Athelstan's mind and changed the law. If there had been a Saxon newspaper in the Dark Ages then it may have broken the news like this …

BINGO

Saxon Times

12 August 927

STILL ONLY HALF A GROAT OR HALF A GOAT

KING'S KINDNESS TO KENT KID!

The people of Maidstone in Kent were cheated of their sport today by King Athelstan. The king got to hear of the case of sheep-rustling Edward Medway. We reported last week how the shepherd killed one of his own sheep and ate its leg. He said the sheep was killed by wolves but the leg had been neatly cut off and its throat slit. As the Maidstone magistrate said, 'I've never seen a wolf that carries a knife!'

The magistrate then sentenced the sheep-slasher to hang by the neck, today at noon. Crowds had gathered from around the county and a fair had been set up in the square around the gallows. Then came the sensational news! King Athelstan has changed the law so crafty criminals like evil Ed can't be killed!

The king wrote to Bishop Theodred and said, 'It is not fair that a man should die so young. Or for such a small offence when he has seen others get away with it elsewhere.' The new law says that no one can be executed if they are under sixteen years of age.

Edward Medway, of course, is twelve years old. But the *Saxon Times* says, 'If he's old enough to steal a sheep he's old enough to swing for it!' We'll soon have fourteen- and fifteen-year-olds getting away with murder!

The only killer kids who can be executed are those that try to fight their way out of being arrested or who run away. Sadly Ed Med did not try to fight or run so the Maidstone holiday crowds went home disappointed.

No hanging today!

Of course there wasn't a Saxon newspaper – there weren't enough people who could read. But the tale of the hungry shepherd is true and shows just how desperate some people could get.

Vile verse

The Saxons had no television. (Even if they had, it would have been useless because they had no electricity to switch it on.) So they entertained themselves with riddles and long stories to pass the long winter nights.

Rotten riddles

One of the most popular pastimes was creating 'riddles' for friends to solve. A riddle was usually told as if it was an object 'speaking' …

Q: I hang between sky and earth; I grow hot from fires and bubble like a whirlpool. What am I?

A: A cooking pot hanging over a fire.

Children did it, adults did it and even the monks did it. Here are some more Saxon riddles …

Q: On the way to a miracle water becomes bone.

A: Ice.

Q: I watched four fair creatures
Travelling together; they left black tracks
behind them. The support of the bird
moved swiftly; it flew in the sky,
dived under the waves.

A: Four fingers and a quill pen.

Q: I am told a certain object grows
In the corner, rises and expands, throws up
a crust. A proud wife carried off
the boneless wonder, the daughter of a king
covered that swollen thing with a cloth.

A: Bread.

Verse and worse

Since Saxons didn't have many books, and so few people could read, most of their stories had to be learned by heart. Now a storyteller can remember a story better if the tale is turned into a poem. Even bits of their history books were written in poetry when the writer got excited about it.

Monster munches

When King Athelstan defeated an army of invading Irish with their savage Scots friends, the Saxons success was recorded in the *Anglo-Saxon Chronicle*. This would be one of the good bits, like the good but gruesome bits you like to hear in your favourite fairy tales – you know the sort of thing: 'Ooooh Grandmama! What big eyes you have!' 'All the better to smell you with.'

Imagine those manic monks sitting round the fire and listening to this part …

The field grew dark with the soldiers' blood
And the corpses were left behind.
The bodies they left to be shared by the beasts
Like the ravens in dusty black coats.
And the grey-coated eagle, the greedy war hawk,
The great grey-haired beast of the forest.

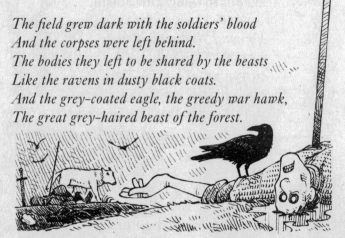

You could try reciting that to someone you don't like, just as they are about to tuck into their school dinner!

As you can see, Saxon poems didn't actually rhyme though. Maybe we can ruin a couple by changing a few words around and making them rhyme ...

Crime story

Today we read crime stories in books and newspapers and we watch them in films or on television. The Saxons' main entertainment was listening to story-poems, so it's not surprising there were crime stories in their poetry. But, being Saxons, the stories were so horrible they'd be given an '18' certificate in the cinema today. You would not want to read such horror, so don't read this updated Saxon poem extract below ...

The Fates of Men

And now he's dead we've hung him up
Upon a roadside gibbet high.
For wicked crimes such men as this
Deserve to suffer and to die.
Such evil men should not live on,
My friends, you must not groan or cry.
See how his helpless hands cannot
Drive off the crows that peck his eyes.

Little Alfie's eyes

Then there was the murder of Prince Alfred in 1036. Poor little Alfie just wanted to be king after the Danish King Cnut died. But Earl Godwin, Saxon Earl of Wessex, had other ideas. This poem based on the *Anglo-Saxon Chronicle* report reveals all ...

Prince Alfred was a cheerful lad, with eyes of sparkling blue,
Till Godwin had his eyes put out. Yes, both! Not one, but two!
He sent the blinded prince away to be a monk in Ely,
There the little Alfie died; did Godwin care? Not really.

Then Godwin set about the slaying of Alf's friends.
He had them caught and had them brought to really sticky ends.
Some he sold as slaves for cash and some he scalped their heads,
Others he locked up in chains and some he killed stone dead.

Some he had their hands chopped off or arms or legs or ears.
No wonder they all fled (or tried to flee) in fear.
We've never seen a crueller deed been done in all our land
Since those dread Vikings came and took peace from our hands.

The Saxons believed that God took revenge on evil doers.
'An eye for an eye', the Bible said. So they would be pleased
to know that Godwin's son, Harold, died at the battle of
Hastings 30 years later ... with an arrow in his eye! And that
was the end of the gruesome Godwins.

Pester your parents

Your parents probably went to school in the days when history was planned to send them to sleep. So they won't know these fascinating facts, the odd things that make history interesting.

Find a parent – you'll probably find one stuck in front of a television – and say, 'Dearest parent, will you either give me ten pounds pocket money or help me with my history homework?' When they say, 'Homework!' then you've got them! Ask these fiendish questions …

1 In England in the 700s what were Noxgagas and Ohtgagas?
a) Instruments of torture that cut off noses and naughty bits.
b) Tribes of people.
c) The Saxon names for carrots and cabbages (or maybe cabbages and carrots).

2 The bitchy monk Alcuin complained to King Offa: 'Some idiot thinks up a new-fangled idea and the next minute the whole country is trying to copy it!' What was he talking about?
a) A new fashion for playing football.
b) A new fashion for a sort of bunjee-jumping with leather ropes.
c) A new fashion for fancy clothes.

3 In 975 King Edgar died suddenly, the harvest was poor and the Saxons starved. What was blamed?
a) A comet appearing in the skies.
b) King Ed walking under a ladder.
c) People not going to church every Sunday.

4 The Britons tried to attack Saxon Athelfrith around AD 603 but were wiped out. What nickname did they give this cunning fighter?
a) The Twister.
b) The Twirler.
c) The Twerp.

5 An assassin stabbed King Edwin of Northumbria with a long dagger. The dagger had to pass through something else first and that saved Edwin. What did the dagger pass through?
a) The wall of the tent where Edwin was sleeping.
b) A Bible that Edwin was carrying.
c) One of Edwin's soldiers.

6 Two cruel young monks discovered the historian Bede was almost blind and played a trick on him. What?
a) They took Bede out to a dangerous cliff, then ran off and left him to find his own way home – or fall off the cliff.
b) They told Bede there was a church full of monks waiting

to hear him preach and led him there. He preached, but the church was empty.

c) They pretended to read a letter to Bede that said his brother was dead, run over by a mad horse.

7 In 1006 a Scottish army was defeated at Durham. The Scots' heads were cut off and stuck on poles around the castle walls. Durham women offered to do what for the relatives of the dead heads?

a) Wash the heads' faces and comb their hair so they looked nice.

b) Act as scarecrows to stop birds pecking the heads.

c) Chase away the children who were throwing wooden balls at the heads and trying to knock them off .

8 Saxon King Ethelred was plagued by Viking raids. He came up with a way of dealing with his problems. What?

a) He had Viking leaders killed.

b) He had Viking women killed.

c) He had Saxon leaders killed.

9 There was no Saxon soap powder. They made their own detergent from ashes, animal fat and …

a) snot.

b) pee.

c) spit.

10 In 686 the villagers of Jarrow went to the local monastery and brought death to the monks. How?

a) The villagers had the plague.

b) The 'villagers' were really Viking warriors in disguise.

c) The villagers came to muck out the stables, upset a lantern in the straw and burned the monastery to the ground while the monks slept and roasted.

Answers:

1b) These people were part of the Mercian kingdom and lived south of the River Thames. Sadly their names have been forgotten in most histories, along with the Wixnas and Wigestas, the Hurstingas and the Feppingas. And you can no longer call yourself (proudly) a Hicca or a Gifla! The West Willas went with the Wigesta, the Wideringas ... and the wind.

2c) The miserable monk thought everyone should wear plain, boring clothes (like history teachers do today). But kings, queens and their courtiers liked flashy, colourful clothes with brooches and embroidery like Dark Age pop stars. Alcuin wore a habit in a delightful shade of mud brown with a smart rope belt and did not approve of painted posers.

3a) If a comet appeared in the sky it was a sure sign of disaster. One appeared in 1066 and, sure enough, the Saxon kingdom was conquered for good.

4a) Athelfrith was known as the Twister, probably because of the way he whirled his sword and not because he ran a fairground ride in his spare time. In a battle against the Welsh some British monks prayed for the Welsh to win. 'Twister' Athelfrith was upset and butchered the 1,200 unarmed monks before going on to massacre the Welsh.

5c) The assassin, Eumer, said he had a message for Edwin. He came up to the king and drew his dagger. One of Edwin's lords, Lilla, threw himself in front of the king. Eumer's powerful thrust went clean through Lilla and wounded the king. Another lord died before the assassin was finally hacked to death.

6b) Bede (so the story goes) was led to the empty church and began preaching to the empty seats while the two young monks laughed themselves sick. But Bede had the last laugh because the church filled up with angels who came down from heaven to hear the old guy.

7a) The women offered to comb the hair of the dead Scots, but they wanted to be well paid for this – a bit like hairdressers today really.

8c) Ethelred trusted no one. In 1006 he had his Saxon leader in York murdered because he was afraid the man was becoming too powerful. Just to be extra sure he took the man's sons and had their eyes put out.

9b) It's supposed to work but don't try this at home. If human pee is such a good cleaner then how come babies nappies are so disgusting when they're full of the stuff?

10a) Most people think of the plague as arriving with the Black Death in 1349, but there were deadly diseases long before that. When the sickness reached Jarrow the villagers flocked to the monastery to get the herbs and cures the monks made. The villagers died and the monks caught the plague from them. Only two monks survived. So much for helping your neighbours!

Epilogue

You can blame the Saxons for a lot.

The monk Bede practically invented English history. Other writers had written about events in the past but Bede sorted them out into some sort of order and gave them dates. As a result history teachers have something to test you on.

Bede would be delighted that we still follow his system.

You can blame him for the Millennium, by the way. Bede sorted out the calendar for you. People used to work out the year by the reign of the monarch ... so the year 2000, say, would have been 'the 47th year of Elizabeth II's reign'. Bede preferred to work time out from the date of the birth of Jesus. So he did. And we still do. Bede would be proud.

And, of course, Bede said the world was round when everyone else thought it was flat. And some sad people (like geography teachers and science teachers) still believe that round-earth nonsense when sensible people like you can see quite plainly that it isn't! But Bede would be pleased.

Then there was the Saxon King Alfred. He reckoned that the Saxons suffered Viking attacks because they had behaved badly. Viking raids were God's punishment. He said the only way for people to be better was to learn more – and people still believe it, so Alfred is partly to blame for you having to go to school and he'd be burning cakes with happiness to see you suffering there!

Athelstan was the first king to make the whole of Britain one country, and it still is – until those Scots in the north get their independence. Athelstan would be chuffed.

Of course the nasty Normans came along and the sad Saxons were defeated. But the Saxon language lived on – which is why you're reading this book in a sort of Saxon English and not Norman French.

King Offa would be pleased at that.

So, thank you Offa, Alfred, Athelstan, and Bede – but a special thanks to those ordinary Saxons whose names never went down in history books. You struggled and died, and made life better for those who came after you.

Smashing Saxons every one.

THE STORMIN'
NORMANS

To John Goddard – a true Blue.

INTRODUCTION

History can be horrible because *people* can be horrible. Well, *most* people can be horrible *some* of the time ... even you. And *some* people can be horrible *most* of the time ... school bullies, school teachers and school children who pull the wings off flies.

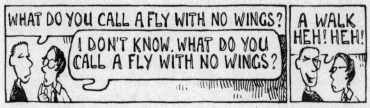

Then there are people who are *paid* to be horrible and torture innocent humans ... tax collectors, traffic wardens and school dinner ladies...

And soldiers. Soldiers can be horrible because it's their job to kill their enemy – if they didn't the enemy would probably try to kill them. You can't go to war and behave like a gentleman, can you?

Some people in the past spent their whole lives fighting wars, so you can imagine how vicious they became. People like the Normans had to be really nasty.

The stormin' Normans were squidged into a corner of northern France and wanted to spread out – get more land. So they fought their way out. And it worked!

Some Normans, like William the Conqueror, hardly ever lost a battle. How did he do it? By being nastier than his enemies.

So you too can learn how to fight back with the help of a few lessons from the stormin' Normans. But be warned – you may become rich and successful, but you'll not be very popular. You will be remembered in history with hatred!

You have been warned!

TIMELINE

911 Charles the Simple, King of France, gives land in Northern France to the Viking Rollo and his people. Their nervous new neighbours call them 'North-men' ... that becomes 'nor-men' ... and finally Normans, geddit?

1017 The Normans set off to conquer the south of Italy. And the Italians have invited them! They've asked the Normans in to keep out some other invaders.

1047 William of Normandy, aged 19, wins his first great battle at Val-es-Dunes on the Norman border with France. Watch out for this teen terror.

1061 Normans begin their conquest of Sicily – but it will take them 30 years to complete because they are always outnumbered.

1066 William of Normandy defeats the English King Harold at the Battle of Hastings. He is crowned King of England and his Norman soldiers settle there.

1084 Germans attack Rome. Normans save the Pope and drive back the Germans – the Normans then raid Rome themselves. Well why not? They'd saved it for a rainy day.

1085 William the Conqueror orders the Domesday Book – a survey of everything everyone in England owns ... so he can have a share. (Today's government still does that.) A year later he dies and Norman William II takes the throne.

1095 Pope Urban II suggests that Christian knights should capture Jerusalem from the Muslims and give it to the Christian Church. Most of Europe agrees but the Normans lead the way. Great excuse to fight with God on their side.

1099 The Crusaders finally capture Jerusalem. With God on their side they massacre the Muslim men, women and children they find there.

1100 The Normans who remain in Jerusalem carve out a new Norman kingdom in the Middle East and call it their Holy Land. Meanwhile back in England William II is killed in a hunting accident ... or was it murder? Brother Henry I takes over.

1119 Henry I's only son dies in a shipwreck. There will be a long and nasty scrap to decide who gets his throne when he dies, which he does in...

1135 Henry I has chosen nephew Stephen to be the next king. Henry's

daughter, Empress Matilda, says, 'I'll fight you for the crown!' The wars bring almost 20 years of misery to England. These times are known as 'The Anarchy'.

1153 War ends when Stephen agrees that Matilda's son can have the throne when he dies. A year later Stephen keeps his promise – and dies. Peace at last.

1154 Henry II of England is from Anjou – an area in France to the south of Normandy. The Norman lords in England are no longer calling themselves Normans, but 'English'.

1199 Big Bad John becomes King of England and Duke of Normandy. But he isn't nicknamed 'Lack-land' for nothing…

1204 French King Philip II takes Normandy. The Normans in England have to choose – do they stay and become English? Or join the French to keep their Norman lands but lose their English ones? Most stay in England. The Normans become English or French but Norman no more.

BIG BAD BILL

GRRR

Of all the Normans, William of Normandy (1028–1087) has to be the most famous, known to the world as William the Conqueror. Bill became Duke of Normandy at the age of 7 and had a scary childhood, always in danger of being murdered by people who wanted his land. He grew up tough enough not only to survive, but to be the first Norman to become a king when he conquered England.

Terrible teen

Bill's first major battle was in 1047, at Val-es-Dunes, at the age of just 19. Historian William of Poitiers said:

> *Young William was not scared at the sight of the enemy swords. He hurled himself at his enemies and terrified them with slaughter. Some of the enemy met their death on the field of battle, some were crushed and trampled in the rush to flee and many horsemen were drowned as they tried to cross the river Orne.*

SPLASH, GURGLE, PUSH, SHOVE, HACK, CHOP!

William later marched on the town of Alençon. The defenders barred its gates and then made fun of his mother's peasant family. They cried:

Leather! Leather for the leather-worker's grandson!

William was furious. When he eventually captured the town he took 32 of the leading citizens of Alençon and paraded them in front of the townsfolk. Then he had their hands and feet cut off.

C'MON BILL! IT WAS JUST A BIT OF FUN!

Mrs Conqueror

William married Matilda in about 1052 or 1053. She was a tiny woman (about 127 cm), but tough, and proved to be a loyal and clever wife.

SHE'S MY BETTER HALF!

VERY FUNNY

You have to sort the facts from the fiction about Matilda though! French historians told the following story…

William was visiting Count Baldwin V when he fell in love with his daughter, Matilda. He asked if he could marry the girl but Matilda herself refused. She sneered…

William secretly went to her house at night where he beat her and kicked her. As the mauled Matilda lay battered on her bed she changed her mind. She said …

The story is probably not true. The Normans were trying to show that their women loved violent men – because that's what the men wanted to believe!

Bill's last battle

William was back in France, attacking the town of Mantes, when he had his last illness. He'd had the town burned to the ground and (one story says) his horse was frightened by the shower of sparks.

The horse stumbled, William slammed his stomach against the front of his saddle and burst his fat gut. He died five weeks later after suffering in agony. Before he died he handed his crown and sword to his son William Rufus. But the moment he died the Norman lords panicked. With the

Conqueror dead there could be rebellions in their lands. Orderic Vitalis, writing 50 years after the death, described what happened next...

> *As soon as William died, the richest of the Norman lords mounted their horses and hurried off to defend their castles. The servants – seeing that their masters had disappeared – laid their hands on the weapons, the gold and silver plate, the rich cloth and the royal furniture. The corpse of the king was left almost naked on the floor.*

The disappearing conqueror

William's body was eventually taken to Caen to be buried in the cathedral William had founded. The journey to the church was interrupted by a fire in the town – they dropped the body, fought the fire, then carried on.

Later the funeral service was interrupted by a local man who said...

THE GROUND WHERE YOU'RE BURYING WILLIAM BELONGS TO ME! I WANT TO BE PAID BEFORE YOU PUT HIM IN THE GRAVE!

He was paid!

Then the clumsy undertakers tried to cram the fat body into a small stone coffin and bits fell off. The smell was so disgusting the bishop rushed through the burial service and everyone ran for it.

Rest in peace, William? No. Only until 1522. In that year the curious Catholic Church had the tomb opened to inspect the body.

Rest in peace, William? No. Only until 1562. In that year Protestants raided the church, broke open tombs and scattered skeletons. All that was left was Will's thigh bone. That was re-buried and a fine monument was built.

Rest in peace, William's thigh bone? No. Only until 1792 when the French Revolution mobs demolished his monument.

Rest in peace, William? For the moment. A simple stone slab now marks the spot where he was buried.

But what happened to that thigh bone? Some say the 1792 rioters threw it out – some say it's still there. Perhaps someone should open the tomb again and find out!

UNLIKELY LEGENDS

Historians have a tough time trying to sort out the truth. They may come across stories in old scripts, but those stories could be untrue.

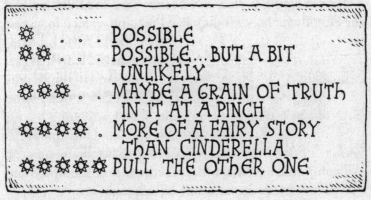

...then in 1075 I went to the moon with the Pope.

Here are a few tales from Norman days that may have some truth in them (one-star porkies) – or may be just legends (five-star whacking great fibs). What would you make of these tales?

✿ . . . . POSSIBLE
✿✿ . . . POSSIBLE...BUT A BIT UNLIKELY
✿✿✿ . . MAYBE A GRAIN OF TRUTH IN IT AT A PINCH
✿✿✿✿ . MORE OF A FAIRY STORY THAN CINDERELLA
✿✿✿✿✿ PULL THE OTHER ONE

Norman nonsense?

1 William the Conqueror's dad, Duke Robert, met his mum, Herleve, while she was dancing in the road. He fell in love with her. Of course this is quite possible – unlike today when dancing in a road would get you a) arrested or b) flattened by a flying Ford Fiesta. ✿✿ *STARS*.

2 Before William the Conqueror was born his mother had a dream. She dreamed a tree was growing from her and the shade of the tree covered Normandy and England. (Just as

143

the son that would grow from her would cast his shadow over Normandy and England. Geddit?) Nowadays her doctor would tell her the bad dreams mean a) nothing or b) she's been eating toasted cheese sandwiches before going to bed.

✿✿✿✿✿ STARS

3 William the Conqueror was tormented by enemies who said he was just the son of a tanner's daughter – a tanner turns animal skins into leather. His grandfather, Fulbert, lived in Falaise where there were a lot of leather-makers, so it is possible. But another story says Fulbert had the charming job of preparing corpses for burial – tidying them up and dressing them.

I THINK YOU'LL LOOK FABULOUS IN THE BLUE TUNIC AND BROWN LEGGINGS

William would have liked that because a) it's a steady job and b) William could go out and kill enough people to keep Grandpa rushed off his feet! ✿ STAR

4 Rollo the Viking was offered the land of Normandy by Charles the Simple in 910. 'Let's make a deal,' Charles said (simply). 'You Vikings can simply have Normandy but I simply insist on being your king. You must simply do homage to me. To show you accept me as king you must simply kiss my foot.' Rollo didn't fancy that much … would you? So he sent one of his soldiers to kiss Charlie's foot. The soldier didn't want to grovel so he grasped the king's foot and lifted

it up to his lips. Of course this tipped Charles the Simple's throne back and he was simply thrown to the ground.

Big laughs for Rollo who was probably a) rolling with laughter or b) Rollo-ing with laughter. ✿✿✿ STARS

5 William the Conqueror was just a teenage duke when he was visiting the castle of one of his lords. He was tipped off that the lord planned to kill him. William escaped from the castle in darkness, rode for 16 hours through the night and came to the wide estuary of the Vire river. He was able to cross it because the tide was out (very lucky) and reached the castle of a friend before he could be caught. He was lucky that a) his horse didn't stumble on dark, uneven roads and break two necks and six legs (William's AND the horse's, if you hadn't worked it out, dummy) or b) he didn't get stopped for speeding by policemen with radar guns. ✿✿ STARS

6 In 1064 Harold Godwinson of England was the man most likely to take the English throne when Edward the Confessor died (which he did in 1066). The story goes that Harold was crossing the English Channel when his ship was caught in a storm. Harold was recognized and taken to William of Normandy (who also fancied himself as King of England when old Ed kicked the bucket). Harold had to promise he would let William become king when Ed died. William set him free … and Harold broke his promise in 1066. But is the story true? Would Harold *really* give away his kingdom?

This is a story told by Norman historians who want to show that a) Harold was a rotten cheat who broke his promises and b) William was the rightful king of England – he wasn't 'William the Conqueror' in 1066, he was 'William the I've-just-popped-over-the-Channel-to-take-what-is-rightfully-mine-old-chap'. ✿ STAR

Odd English

If the Normans had some strange beliefs, the English people had some stories that were even stranger!

1 In 1080 a man called Eadulf died in the village of Ravensworth in northern England. His relatives came to watch over the corpse but they were shocked when Eadulf sat up and said, 'Don't be afraid! I have risen from the dead. Make the sign of the cross on yourselves and on the house.' When they'd done that the house was filled with birds that flew in everyone's faces till a priest sprinkled them with holy water. Eadulf said, 'I've visited Hell, where I've seen the wicked tortured, and Heaven where I've seen a few old friends.' He also warned, 'I've seen places being prepared in Hell for some living people! One of them was Waltheof – English Earl of Northumberland.'

Shortly after this Waltheof became the only English leader to be executed by William the Conqueror. Weird? Or wacky?

✿✿✿✿✿ STARS

2 An English rebel, Edric the Wild, tried to make trouble for William the Conqueror in 1067. This Edric went out for a stroll after dinner one evening and came across a group of fairies dancing. Edric fell in love with one of these little ladies and married her. When Edric was defeated William the Conqueror ordered that this fairy wife should be brought to court so he could meet her. What on earth would big bullying Bill say to a fairy? 'Lend us your wand'?

✿✿✿✿✿ STARS

3 King Harold was slaughtered at the Battle of Hastings in 1066. But the English told a story that he survived the battle, buried under a pile of bodies. A peasant woman found him and nursed him back to health. He hid in a cellar in Winchester for two years before leading attacks on the hated Normans. In time he got religion and became Harold the hermit. Many English would love to believe their last great hero survived. Dream on. Just a little more possible than fairies. ✿✿✿✿ STARS

Painful poisoners

The Norman historians had a thing about poison! If someone died suddenly then they said, 'It could well have been poison!' Here are a few curious cases for you to judge, Sherlock...

1 William the Conqueror invited Count Conan of Brittany to join him in the conquest of England in 1066. Count Conan said:

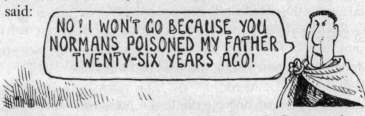

NO! I WON'T GO BECAUSE YOU NORMANS POISONED MY FATHER TWENTY-SIX YEARS AGO!

The story goes that William decided to settle Conan and got one of Conan's lords to take the count's hunting horn and gloves. These were smeared with poison. When Count Conan went hunting he wiped his mouth with the poisoned glove and died. He was really out for the count!

COUNT DOWN

Was William really guilty of this murder? Possibly, though Conan died two months after the Normans landed at Hastings.

It's a lesson to us all: a) don't wipe your mouth on the back of your glove or b) get your teacher to taste your gloves before you put them on.

2 In 1060 Robert of Gere came to a nasty and suspicious end. Norman historian Orderic wrote...

> One day Robert was sitting happily by the fire and watched his wife holding four apples in her hand. He playfully snatched two from her and didn't realize that they were poisoned. He ate them though his wife told him not to. The poison took effect and after five days he died.

Again it's possible that he *was* poisoned.

And another lesson: **a)** do what your wife tells you or **b)** don't snatch food from someone else's hand … especially if you don't know when they last washed that hand!

3 Lady Mabel of Belleme plotted to poison her husband's enemy, Arnold of Echauffour, who was visiting them. She placed a poisoned goblet of wine on the table and waited. Unfortunately her brother-in-law, Gilbert, came in sweaty and hot from hunting. He cried…

…snatched up the poisoned cup and swallowed the lot.

He died.

Now, if you'd been Mabel, you'd have given up, wouldn't you? Not her. She bribed one of enemy Arnold's servants to put poison in his food, which he did. Arnold died. Second time lucky!

A lesson there: **a)** if at first you don't succeed, try again or **b)** don't take wine from Mabel's table (or read the label if you're able).

4 Lady Mabel then survived a poison plot against herself. The monks of Saint Evroul were fed up with her visiting them with dozens of servants to eat all their best food.

She returned, and ate ... and fell ill. She ordered that her baby be brought to her for feeding. She let the baby suck milk at her breasts. The baby died. (From poison in his mother's body?)

And Mabel? She survived.

A lesson for us all: **a)** don't go where you're not wanted and **b)** don't have a murdering meanie like Mabel for a mother!

5 William the Conqueror's dad (Robert) became Duke of Normandy only after his older brother (Richard) died suddenly. Many people believed that William's dad had poisoned his uncle in order to get his hands on Normandy.

If Robert was poisoned a few years later (and some say he was) then he must have died thinking...

The lesson seems to be: *never* trust *any* Norman who offers you food or drink!

Of course Norman cooks weren't too fussy about washing their hands after using the toilet or picking their scabs or patting a dog. They didn't know about germs and hygiene. A lot of people in those days must have died from germs in their food that gave them food poisoning.

1066 AND ALL THIS

1066 was a funny old year. It saw three kings in England and three great battles. And if the year 1066 had kept its own diary[1] it would have been packed with horrible history...

1 January

Happy New Year, everyone in England! Edward the Confessor is King of England. But he's a poorly man. Old Ed has no children and no one's very sure about who'll get the throne when he dies. There are a lot of English people who are nervous about the coming year. Harold Godwinson for one — he is the most powerful lord in England. He practically rules the south for Edward the Confessor while his brother, Tostig Godwinson, rules the north.

Harold is a tough nut. For years the Welsh had been a problem . . . until Edward the Confessor sent Harold off to sort them out in 1063. Here's what happened. . .

THE FIGHTING WAS VICIOUS. THE WELSH SENT HAROLD SEVERED HEADS TO SHOW THEY TOOK NO PRISONERS. HAROLD DIDN'T MIND PLAYING BY THOSE RULES.

A WELSH PRISONER? EXECUTE HIM.

THE WELSH WERE SO BATTERED THEY TURNED AGAINST THEIR OWN LEADER, GRUFFYDD, AND BEGGED HAROLD FOR PEACE. HE TOLD THEM...

YOU CAN HAVE PEACE WHEN YOU BRING ME THE HEAD OF GRUFFYDD.

1. To be honest there is a diary that was kept by monks called *The Anglo-Saxon Chronicle* but it's got lots of boring bits.

152

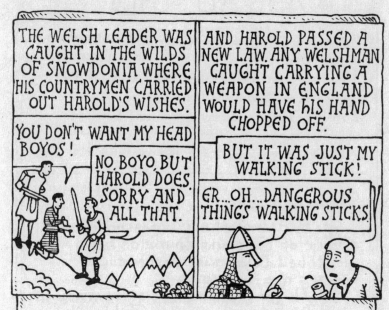

THE WELSH LEADER WAS CAUGHT IN THE WILDS OF SNOWDONIA WHERE HIS COUNTRYMEN CARRIED OUT HAROLD'S WISHES.

YOU DON'T WANT MY HEAD BOYOS!

NO, BOYO, BUT HAROLD DOES. SORRY AND ALL THAT.

AND HAROLD PASSED A NEW LAW. ANY WELSHMAN CAUGHT CARRYING A WEAPON IN ENGLAND WOULD HAVE HIS HAND CHOPPED OFF.

BUT IT WAS JUST MY WALKING STICK!

ER...OH...DANGEROUS THINGS WALKING STICKS!

So Harold is a great warrior and the English army is in pretty good shape. I've a feeling it will need to be.

5 January
Edward the Confessor died. (I told you he was poorly, didn't I? You don't get much more poorly than that!)

6 January
Edward was buried today. That's a bit quick! His body can hardly be cold! And Harold Godwinson is crowned king. He didn't hang around did he? It will all end in tears, you mark my words.

February
That William of Normandy is upset! He's sent some of his

lords over to England with a message for King Harold. The message says. . .

1 Two years ago you promised that I would be King of England when Edward the Confessor died.

2 We also agreed that your sister would marry my son, while you married my sister.

Harold's reply is brief and to the point. . .

Dear William,

Edward the Confessor left the throne of England to me on his deathbed. We must respect the wishes of a dying man.

As for exchanging sisters I regret that I am now married to Ealdgyth. And I regret even more that my sister cannot marry your son since she has died. Perhaps you'd like me to send her corpse across to Normandy?

Harold (King of England)

I have heard that William has started building two thousand ships to invade England. There'll be trouble now!

24 April

Amazing! Fantastic and spooky! A comet has appeared in the skies over England! It's like a brilliant star with a tail. We all know it's a sign of a great disaster. The trouble is no one knows who will suffer the disaster – the English or the Normans. The English lords are telling Harold he should invade Normandy and put a stop to Wicked William's plans, but he won't do it.

WHEN WILLIAM SETS SAIL WE'LL JUST SINK HIS SHIPS. WE'VE A STRONG NAVY. EASY.

May

Would you believe it? An invasion on the south coast and the navy was away in the north!! Were the invaders sent by that William of Normandy? No, they were led by Harold's own brother . . . treacherous Tostig. As soon as Harold marched from London to fight him, Tostig jumped in his boat and sailed away. They reckon he's doing a deal with the Viking they call Hardrada – Hard Ruler – for the two of them to attack the north of England. Poor Harold won't know if he's coming or going! But he will know who his friends are, and they don't include Wicked William, Horrible Hardrada or Terrible Tostig!

August

Still no sign of those Normans. Some say they're waiting for the right wind to carry their ships over the Channel.

8 September

Oh dear! Oh dear! Oh dear! Harold's army couldn't wait on the south coast for ever. They've had to go home to help with the harvest. But the navy's been sent to London and some terrible storms have wrecked a lot of them. I hope that Wicked William doesn't decide to come now!

They say William has lost a lot of ships in the same storms. Norman bodies were washed ashore and he had them buried secretly so the rest of the troops wouldn't be upset. Wimps. They'll never beat Heroic Harold even if they do get across the Channel!

20 September

Hardrada is here! He landed in Yorkshire and drew first blood. When I say blood I mean blood! Our Harold wasn't there so Hardrada attacked his earls. The English were driven into the marshes at Fulford near York and slaughtered. There were so many bodies the Vikings were able to cross the marsh by stepping on corpses like stepping-stones!

Now Horrible Hardrada wants food and drink from the people of York. He makes a terrible demand. . .

TO THE PEOPLE OF YORK,

WE WANT BREAD AND WE WANT WINE. SO THAT YOU DON'T BETRAY US I WANT 150 CHILDREN FROM YORK AS MY PRISONERS. MY MEN WILL COLLECT THEM FROM STAMFORD BRIDGE THIS MONDAY 25th. BE THERE OR BEWARE!

HARDRADA

25 September

What a day! Hardrada and Tostig turned up to collect their hostages at Stamford Bridge. But they had less than half of their army and they didn't have all their weapons! Guess who turned up to spoil their party? Our heroic Harold!

Harold made an offer to his brother Tostig.

And what a fight it was! A Viking hero blocked the bridge and slew 40 English before they could cross. The English sent a boat under the bridge, pushed a pike through the planks and stabbed him from below.

Harold's men swarmed over the Vikings. Hardrada, with little armour on, took an arrow in the windpipe and died. Tostig was hacked down when he refused to surrender.

Harold's English have defeated the invaders. The man is unbeatable! Now he is heading south just in case Wicked William lands there. He leaves his exhausted northern army behind. He'll have fresh men from the south if he needs them.

28 September

It's all happening this week! William the Norman has landed with his army on the south coast as Harold rides to meet him. That Wicked William was soon spreading stories about Harold. . .

DID YOU KNOW YOUR EVIL HAROLD KILLED HIS BROTHER TOSTIG AND SLICED ThE HEAD OFF THE CORPSE?

14 October

Gallant Harold finally came face to face with Duke William today near Hastings. And that's where Harold will be staying. The English fought all day but in the end the Norman knights and archers destroyed them. They say Harold was wounded in the eye and cut to pieces by William's knights. There is even a story that Wicked William himself had a chop or two at the corpse. Harold's brothers died with him. So mark today in your calendars for all time. It's the end of Saxon England and the start of Norman England.

15 October

King Harold's corpse has been taken to the seashore and buried under a pile of stones. The cruel conqueror William refused to give him a Christian burial. But he did give him a headstone reading:

HAROLD, YOU REST HERE, TO GUARD THE SEA AND SHORE

October

William and the Normans have been taking town after town as they march to London. The English have no castles to make it harder for William. But William and his Normans were almost stopped by something they got from Canterbury . . . the disease of dysentery. William and his soldiers are starting to fall sick with vomiting, fever and diarrhoea with blood. Some die but William lives.

November

London has surrendered and begs William to take the crown.

25 December

It's 'Happy Christmas, Your Grace', as Duke William was crowned King of England. The cheers of his Normans inside Westminster Abbey made the soldiers outside think there was a riot. They started burning and looting the city. William was crowned amidst flames! Still, this is what we'll have to expect now the Normans are in charge.

31 December

Goodbye from 1066. And many happy New Years to you all. You'll forget many things in your lifetime, but you'll never forget heroic Harold, William the Conqueror or me . . . 1066.

LIVE LIKE A NORMAN

Name that Norman

The Normans' Viking ancestors often gave their people nicknames but they didn't always call people the nicknames to their face. Harold Bluetooth may not have minded you using his nickname too much. But you'd probably have got a clout from Olaf the Stout!

The Normans carried on this habit with some of their leaders. Duke William's mother wasn't married to his father so his enemies called him William the Bastard ... his friends (and sensible people) called him William the Conqueror.

Can you match the nicknames to these Normans?

Of course the meanest-sounding nickname went to the French king who invited the Vikings into Normandy in the first place – he was Charles the Simple. But in those days 'simple' meant 'pure' rather than stupid. Simple, isn't it?

Eat like a Norman

The Norman recipes we have are not very detailed. If you want to taste Norman-type food then you have to work a lot of it out for yourself – how much to put in each mixture and how long to cook it.

Here's a Norman dish you may like to try. It was probably eaten by the rich Normans and not their poor peasant farmers. If it doesn't work very well then have a cat or dog handy to help you eat it.

161

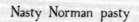

Nasty Norman pasty

You need:
Meat
Eggs
Cheese
Pastry

To make:
Boil the meat in a pan of water till it is cooked.
Make pastry and roll it out.
Chop up the cooked meat, beat the eggs and grate the cheese then stir them together.
Make the mixture into balls about the size of apples.
Wrap each ball in pastry.
Bake in a hot oven till the pastry is golden brown.

To serve:
Place on a wooden plate and eat with a knife and fingers.

Remember to get an adult to do the sharp knife bits and the boiling water stuff. It is much more fun to watch an adult chop their scalded fingers off than it is to chop your own. After all, you probably need your fingers to pick your nose, don't you?

It shouldn't kill you ... though it is best to remember: the Normans ate this and they are all dead!

Salty science
Of course your meal will taste better with salt in it. In Norman times you couldn't pop along to the local

supermarket and buy a packet. To get some in your salt cellar you had to buy it from a salt seller.

Where did the salt seller get his salt?

Sometimes salt was dug from pits in the ground and you could make a lot of money if you owned a salt mine …

WHAT DID THE MISERLY PIT-OWNER SAY WHEN HE LOOKED AT HIS SALT PITS?

I DON'T KNOW, WHAT DID THE MISERLY PIT-OWNER SAY WHEN HE LOOKED AT HIS SALT PITS?

MINE! ALL MINE!

But if you lived close to the coast and wanted to save some money then you could make your own salt from sea water. The Normans knew enough science to be able to do it.

POOR WOMAN'S WEEKLY

Salt that supper

Want to give your family a real treat tonight? Then sprinkle their food with salt, fresh from the sea! Simply fill a pot with sea water and set it to boil.

When the water's boiled away the salt will have formed a white crust around the pot. Wait till it cools – you don't want to burn those lovely hands, do you? Then scrape the salt from the sides of the pot and store it in a cool dry place till you need it. Scrummy!

Horrible Histories Health Warning: Don't try this at home. Sea water in the 2000s isn't as pure as it was in the 1000s!

As well as flavouring food, salt could be used to preserve it. In the days before fridges meat could be covered in salt to stop it going bad.

This was useful in the Norman world. There wasn't usually enough grass to keep all the animals over the winter. So any spare animals were killed and the meat salted. Would you enjoy the job of deciding which of those sweet little calves and lambs and piglets should feel father's axe?

Dazzling dressers

Peacocks have the fancy feathers and the terrific tails. Peahens look boring alongside them. And it was a bit like that in Norman times. It was the rich men who were the flashy dressers.

Peculiar 'poulaines'

Norman soldiers probably invented 'poulaines' – the famous shoes that had long, pointed toes. In time the toes curled up in great loops and had to be chained to the knee to stop the flop.

But in Norman times there was a story that the shoes were invented by Fulk, Duke of Anjou. (Anjou is just a bit to the south of Normandy.) The story goes that Fulk had a lump growing on his foot and he designed the shoes to hide the fact he had an ugly foot. It's possible that Fulk did wear the shoes but he probably didn't 'invent' them – he just borrowed the idea from his knightly Norman neighbours.

WARNING: Do not read the following if you are easily shocked or need a sense of humour transplant. Two hundred and fifty years after Fulk invented (or didn't invent) 'poulaines' they were turned into something quite disgraceful by some Frenchmen. They stuffed the long toes with sawdust and shaped them to look like a man's naughty bits. The French king Charles V banned such rude shoes in 1367.

True or false

History can be horribly difficult. Even a history teacher would struggle to get ten out of ten with these quick but quirky questions. Try these on some sad teacher, get them to answer true or false, and see who will be the conqueror...

1 A Norman boy could became a monk at the age of seven and would never be able to give up the monastery.

2 The Normans ate canaries on toast.

3 The Domesday Book wasn't called the Domesday Book.

4 Some Norman women used the poisonous deadly nightshade plant to make their eyes more attractive.

5 Norman minstrels played bagpipes.

6 Norman town houses had kitchens next to the dining room so the food stayed hot.

7 A Norman knight slept better in his tent if he had a dolly over his head.

8 The Normans enjoyed Easter eggs.

9 The Normans always built their castles on waste land so no one lost fields or houses.

10 Normans on the coast had a lifeboat rescue service for ships in the English Channel.

Answers:

1 False. Before the Normans invaded England it had been true that boys took vows at the age of seven that could never be broken. If they did leave the monastery then they became outlaws. But the Normans changed this. Boys spent nine years in the monastery and, at the end of that time, they could leave – or stay for ever. But there was a catch in some monasteries. If you left before the age of 16 you might have to pay the monks for what they had taught you! Imagine that! Having to pay to leave school!

2 False. The Normans brought canaries from the Canary Islands (believe it or not). The Canary Islanders loved to eat the little feathered foodstuff but the Normans wanted them for their singing.

3 True. A hundred years after it was written the book was nicknamed the 'Domesday Book' because it was like the Christian Day of Judgement (Doomsday) in that there could be no appeal against it. You were stuck with what the book said about your land and your wealth. The book called itself a 'descriptio' which is a Latin word meaning a 'writing down'. It was kept in the Royal Treasury at Winchester and the early Normans knew it as 'The Winchester Book'. (No prizes for guessing why.) By 1170 people were calling it 'Domesday' and as late as the 1900s it was still being used to settle arguments over who owned what. Bet your school exercise books don't last that long!

4 True. But very rarely! Norman women in Western Europe used hardly any make-up. Rich women in Eastern Europe used lip colour and drops of deadly nightshade to make the black centre of the eyes (the pupils) open wide. Gorgeous.

5 True. The Normans enjoyed good music (which makes you wonder why they liked the bagpipes). With harps, fiddles, flutes, cymbals, bassoons, trombones and trumpets they could have tortured your eardrums till they burst.

6 False. The houses were made of wood and the roofs were thatched with reeds. If they caught fire the house could be destroyed in half an hour. Kitchens were built separately from the house so there was less chance of careless cooks setting the house on fire. Food would not be so hot when it reached the table. Better a cool dinner than a hot house, they reckoned.

7 True. The tent pole went through a hole in the roof – called an 'onion'! To stop the rain coming through the gap between pole and hole a cap was put on top. This cap was called a 'dolly'.

8 True. During Lent (the weeks before Easter) the Church did not allow Christians to eat eggs. So housewives would save up all their eggs to have as a special treat on Easter Day. They would be boiled and coloured with natural dye – try boiling an egg with onion skins and see what happens! Have your boiled eggs blessed by a priest and scoff them. Sorry – no chocolate eggs, fat face.

9 False. The Normans sometimes found new sites for their castles but they often built them slap bang in the middle of a town. And what do you usually have in the middle of a town? That's right, houses. What happened to the houses? The people were thrown out and they were flattened – 160 homes in Lincoln and another hundred in Norwich, for example. Eudo Dapifer built a castle at Eaton Socon over a church and graveyard. Spooky, eh?

10 False. Quite the opposite! In 1046 a fleet from Flanders was storm-damaged in the English Channel. People from the Norman coast villages hurried to the beaches and waved lanterns to guide the ships to the shore. When the storm-bashed sailors landed the villainous villagers massacred them and stole the cargoes from the ships!

TERRIFIC TALES

People in Norman times worked hard from sunrise to sunset – then they stopped because it was too dark to carry on. They were just like you after a hard day at school – they wanted some entertainment.

You turn on the television or the computer or even pick up a book. The Normans had none of these things. What they had were 'jongleurs'. A jongleur was a musician, a juggler, and an acrobat. He was also a story-teller. He recited or sang long story-poems about great heroes like Roland and Oliver.

YOUNG OLIVER AND ROLAND, THEY WENT OFF TO FIGHT IN SPAIN.
THEY FOUGHT AGAINST THE SARACENS BUT GOT BATTERED IN THE BRAIN. TRA LA!
OUR BRAVE YOUNG MEN GOT MASSACRED AND NEVER FOUGHT AGAIN.
THEIR SAD, SAD TALE LEFT THEIR FRIENDS JUST CRYING LIKE A DRAIN. TRA LA!

IT'S SO SAD

Oliver and Roland had been Christian knights and may really have existed. They fought a gallant but hopeless battle against the Saracens (the Norman name for Muslim warriors). The two friends faced a mighty army alone but Roland was too proud to call for help. They were killed, of course. The story was told as an example to Norman crusaders who were urged to copy their bravery.

There is a legend (it may even be true) that a jongleur led William the Conqueror's troops into the Battle of Hastings.

The Norman historian, Wace, said…

> *A minstrel named Taillefer went in front of the Norman army, singing and juggling with his sword while the troops marched behind singing the Song of Roland.*

THEY MUST BE TOUGH IF THEY CAN PUT UP WITH THAT!

Sounds a bit like a bunch of football supporters on their way to a match. We don't know what Harold's English troops sang.

WE LOVE YOU ROLAND, WE DO!
ROLAND DIED AND SO WILL YOU!

Brave Brit 1

When the Normans arrived in England they found the British had their own legends – dead and living. The dead hero was King Arthur. The Normans loved the story of Arthur and their writers and poets turned him from a British warrior into a magical king. Here's how the story grew…

- In 1135 Geoffrey of Monmouth writes about Arthur. (Though another writer at that time says, 'It is quite clear that everything Geoffrey wrote about Arthur was made up.')
- In 1155 a jongleur called Wace tells Arthur's story and added a bit about a Round Table.

- In 1160 Chretien de Troyes adds bits to the story to make Arthur a knight in armour, not just a British warrior.

- In 1190 a poet called Robert be Boron adds the bit about Arthur's knights and the Holy Grail – the cup that Jesus drank from at the last supper. People who drink from that can live for ever.

- Around 1200-ish an English priest adds that Arthur isn't dead, just sleeping. He'll wake up when England is threatened again. (So where was the sleepy old wrinkly when William the Conqueror landed?)

But there's an even stranger story about the discovery of Arthur's tomb at Glastonbury Abbey.

Arthur's grave

In 1184 there was a disaster when Glastonbury Abbey burned down. The monks were poor and were desperate for money. They needed visitors. Tourists! Pilgrims! But how could they attract them?

There was one thing that might help…

Do you know? How could they cash in on that story and make Glastonbury a tourist attraction? Someone had a brilliant idea!

And, would you believe it, when the monastery was being rebuilt Arthur's tomb *was* found there! The monks' story was a good one. They said...

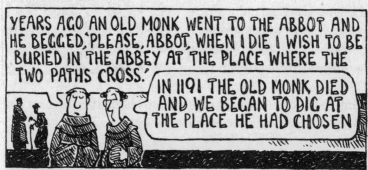

173

Visitors and pilgrims flocked to the Abbey (even the King came to see the grave) and Glastonbury Abbey became the richest monastery in Britain.

But were the monks telling the truth? If you want to make a fortune then find a dead hero in your back garden. After 800 years some people still believe the story of Arthur's burial at Glastonbury! They even believe in his Round Table.

Do you believe it? Or is it just Norman nonsense?

Brave Brit 2

The living legend was the English freedom-fighter, Hereward the Wake. The truth is…

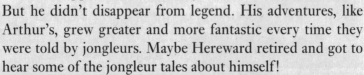

- Hereward went on fighting against William the Conqueror's forces when other English leaders had given up.
- Hereward joined forces with Danish invaders and robbed Peterborough Abbey to stop its riches falling into the hands of the Normans.
- The rebels hid in the marshes where the Normans eventually surrounded and captured them.
- Hereward escaped … and pretty well disappeared from history.

But he didn't disappear from legend. His adventures, like Arthur's, grew greater and more fantastic every time they were told by jongleurs. Maybe Hereward retired and got to hear some of the jongleur tales about himself!

Maybe Hereward's legendary deeds need a new jongleur epic for reciting around the fire at your castle hearth (or your nearest central-heating radiator will do if you don't live in a castle).

Hereward's revenge

My friends I'll sing a song to you, if you your seats will take;
I'll tell you all of our great hero, Hereward the Wake.
He was away from England when the Normans came to Hastings.
And missed the mighty battle where old Harold took a pasting.

Our hero came back home and found his younger brother dead.
'The dirty rotten Normans, they have killed our kid!' he said.
'I'll be revenged, you wait and see, with English help and Dane!'
And off he set to find some ways to bring the Normans pain.

When he arrived at his old house the great hall it was swarmin'
With knights and soldiers all around, each one a deadly
*   Norman.*
'I can't fight fifty men,' he sighed ... our hero was not thick.
'To take them on I need to think of some real clever trick!'

Our Hereward decided as a Norman he would pose,
He pinched a pointy helmet (with that straight bit down the nose).

And then he slipped inside his home where Norman soldiers feasted.
He drank pure English water while the Normans wined and eated.

The bloated Normans fell asleep but Hereward was awake,
He took his knife and slit their throats, 'Take that!' he cried,
   'That take!'
Then Hereward he cut the Norman heads off at the neck.
'I'll teach you Norman nasties to go killing us, by heck!'

Then he found some nails and a hammer (in his garden shed),
And he decorated each doorway with a nasty Norman head.
So no one would come asking him, 'Now whose dead heads are
   those?'
He left their pointy helmets on (with that straight bit down the
   nose).

Some say the Normans caught our hero Hereward the Wake,
One day when he was fast asleep, and his brave life they taked.
But I am sure he still lives on, our Hereward the Wake,
Who found that fighting Norman knights was just a piece of cake.

TRA-LA! TRA-LA! OH FOL-DE-ROL!
TRA-LA! TRA-LA! TRA-LEE!
TRA-LA! TRA-LA! OH FOL-DE-ROL!
I'LL BID YOU ALL GOOD-BYE-EE!

Did you know… ?

Hereward was given the name 'The Wake' because he was always 'watchful'. It didn't mean he was always awake.

He *did* go to sleep but he never slept in a bed! He always slept alongside it. An enemy could have sneaked in while Hereward the Wake wasn't awake. If the enemy attacked the bed then he'd miss Hereward the Wake who'd wake.

Good tip, that, for those of you who go away on school trips.

The knight visitor

Jongleurs had to be paid for their entertaining. They could choose to travel around … then they could sing the same songs over and over again, but they weren't sure when they'd get their next pay-day. The alternative was to stay in one castle … then they became known as minstrels and had to keep coming up with new songs all the time, but at least they were sure of food and shelter.

Generally poor people couldn't afford to hire a jongleur and they didn't have musical instruments themselves. So what could they do to entertain themselves and the kids? Tell stories, of course. Here is a story from Norman times that was told all over Europe. Are you sitting comfortably?

Once upon a time there was a brave young knight called Prince Hugo. There was nothing our young Hugo liked better than doing a bit of embroidery. Hugo made all his own dresses and let his hair grow down to his waist.

'He's a bit ... odd,' the courtiers in his castle whispered to one another. But Hugo had his reasons. He didn't let the gossip needle him.

Hugo could have passed for a girl ... which, as it happened, was exactly what he wanted.

You see, he'd heard about the poor princess Hilde. She was the most beautiful, clever and tragic princess in the whole of Normandy ... maybe even in the whole world. Hilde's father, Count Walgund, had locked her in a tall tower. The tower was in a forest and the forest was infested with the wildest wolves in the west.

Count Walgund was so devoted to his dear daughter that he didn't want to lose his lovely lass to some layabout lout of a lad. He didn't want her running off and getting married – unless it was to a perfect husband.

One day Hugo put on his best frock, embroidered by himself with a squillion sequins he'd sewn on, and arrived at Count Walgund's castle. 'I am a lost lady whose homeland has been conquered by a cruel king. I ask only a bed for the night, good count!'

Before the count could answer, his countess cried, 'Look at that dress! What a work of a needle-woman's wondrous art! You simply must teach our daughter how to embroider like that, mustn't she, Count?'

To say the dress was the work of a woman is, of course, sexist. Countess Walgund wouldn't get away with it today, would she lads? Boys today know their needles from their nine-pound notes, oh dear me, yes! Anyway the daft old bat was wrong because Hugo was a bloke!

Now we know that's exactly what our clever little Hugo was after all the time, don't we? Next day he was in the tower and teaching the lovely Hilde the ropes ... well the threads, if you know what I mean.

Hilde loved her new chum – loved her deep voice, her strong hands, her broad shoulders. 'Excuse me,' Hilde said after a week. 'But would I be correct in thinking that you are really a man disguised as a woman.'

Hugo clicked his long fingers. 'Curses! How did you guess?'

'I think it's probably the beard that gave you away,' Hilde confessed.

Hugo rubbed his rough chin and sighed. 'Sorry. You don't mind, do you?'

179

'Mind!' Hilde cried. 'I'm chuffed to fluffy fairy feathers! I think you're gorgeous!'

'You're not so bad yourself,' Hugo admitted.

Before another week was out they were married. Then Hugo declared, 'I have to leave now. I must find a way to persuade your father that I will make him a good son-in-law.'

'That's a bit sudden, my pet!' Hilde moaned, but she saw the sense in what he said. Hugo chopped his hair, and swapped his female dress for male chain-mail. Off he rode on a crusade where he fought side-by-side with Count Walgund. They were gone a long time. A long, long time ... well, a couple of years anyway ... and things had been happening in the tall tower.

'Come home with me, my brave young friend,' Count Walgund said to Hugo. Now, we know that's exactly what our clever little Hugo was after all the time, don't we?

But as they rode close to the tall tower Walgund saw a wolf cross the path and cried, 'After it! Kill it! We can't have wolves wandering my paths and putting my people in peril!'

So they chased the wolf who turned to face the fierce knights. The wolf dropped a bundle she was carrying and slipped off into the deep dark trees. But the knights saw the white linen bundle wriggling. They stopped and picked it up. It was a baby boy!

'Good grief! Wonder who you belong to, my little man!' Walgund warbled. 'What a wonderful child. Wouldn't mind one like that for my grandson! Let's visit my daughter in a nearby tower. See if she can care for it till we find the rightful mother.'

When they reached the tower and unlocked the door Hilde rushed out.

Was she going to fuss over her father?

Was she going to hug Hugo?

No!

She ran across the courtyard and snatched the baby from the two men and wailed, 'My baby! The washerwoman left the kitchen door open this morning and he crawled off into the forest! I was sure he'd be killed by wolves!'

'Your baby?' Count Walgund said in wonder. 'Who's the father?'

Hilde raised her arm and pointed at Prince Hugo. 'Why, Hugo here!'

The count was confused, you can count on that. But, when he finally understood he happily hugged his daughter, his grandson and his son-in-law.

'What a day!' Hugo sighed. 'I've gained a son I never knew I had.'

'What a day!' Walgund cried. 'I've gained a son and a grandson I never knew I had!'

'I've waited for your return before I named the child,' Hilde said. 'What should we call him?'

Walgund looked at Hugo. Hugo looked at Walgund. The two knights looked at one another. They nodded. They said it together. 'Wolf, of course'.

Hilde and Hugo lived happy hever hafter.

NORMAN WISDOM

Are you as wise as a Norman? To understand the past you have to know how the people *thought*. Here are a few Norman beliefs…

1 *The Normans believed*… that many of their Muslim enemies were cowards. The Normans had won great victories in Europe where their charging knights smashed the enemy to the ground. But when the Norman Crusaders met the Muslim forces they had problems. The Muslims didn't line up and wait to be smashed to the ground! Instead they rode in a circle around the Crusaders and shot arrows at them from a distance.

WHY CAN'T THEY STAND STILL AND BE KILLED LIKE EVERYONE ELSE?

URK

Many Norman knights believed there was a reason for this…

THE MUSLIMS HAVE MORE BLOOD IN THEIR BODIES THAN WE HAVE. THEY ARE AFRAID OF GETTING HURT BECAUSE THEIR BLOOD WILL BURST OUT

Normans later learned to respect their Muslim enemies.

2 *The Normans believed*… that living too long in the Holy Land – what we call the Middle East today – was unhealthy. The hot climate and the strong wine affected the brain. (Of

course the easy answer would be not to drink the wine, but the water could be even more deadly ... and Coca-Cola hadn't been invented.) As a result people back in Europe said...

THE WEATHER OUT THERE MAKES PEOPLE MAD THEN DEAD!

3 *The Normans believed*... that painful punishments were the fairest. If they locked a criminal in jail then the family might starve. That would punish the innocent family. So, instead, they thought it was better to make a public display of the criminal – parade them in the stocks so that everybody could see this was a person not to be trusted. For more serious crimes they could decide to cut a bit off a criminal – a hand or a nose, perhaps. The criminal could then go back to work and support the family!

BUT I'M A HANDY MAN!

4 *The Normans believed*... that God would help them to give justice to criminals. Like the English before them they settled some cases by having a trial by 'ordeal'. A woman accused of theft could be made to hold a red-hot iron bar. Her hand was bandaged. If it healed she was innocent. A

man could be tied up and thrown into water that had been blessed – if he sank he was innocent. (A bit like witch trials of later years.)

5 *The Normans believed…* that God was on their side, especially when they were fighting against the Muslims in Sicily or the Holy Land. The head of the Catholic Church, the Pope, told them, 'Look, lads, it's OK to kill those Muslims. God will forgive you.' So the Norman knights hacked away happily, believing it wasn't murder … even when it was. It wasn't only the Pope who said killing was all right. God sent a messenger from heaven personally! None other than Saint George! At the battle of Cerami in 1063 he turned up to help 130 Normans defeat thousands of Muslims. The soldiers reported…

The Pope believed the story and sent a flag, like the one in the vision, for the Normans to carry into future battles.

Saint George turned up again 35 years later at the battle for Antioch in the Holy Land. An unknown writer said...

> *Our soldiers saw a countless army of men on white horses whose banners were all white. When our men saw this they realized this was help sent by Christ and the leader was Saint George. This is quite true for many of our men saw it.*

Sadly old Georgie wasn't around at Hattin in 1187 when the Crusaders were smashed. Perhaps it was his day off! He then returned a few years later to help Richard the Lionheart win another victory in the Holy Land. Bet the Crusaders wished he'd make his mind up ... or send a letter to let them know he'd be around!

6 *The Normans believed*... that their doctors knew best. In the 1100s a knight was wounded in the leg and the wound became infected. An Arab doctor treated the wound and it started to get better.

it's nothing

An Arab soldier, Usamah Ibn Munqidh described what happened…

Yesterday a doctor arrived from Europe. A small man with a curling brown beard and rather dirty hands 'What are you doing to this knight?' he demanded.

'I am placing a herbal plaster on the wound to help it heal', the Arab doctor said.

'Herbal plaster! Nonsense!' the European doctor snorted. 'You Arabs are ignorant, simple people. You know as much about medicine as I do about the moon.' He turned to the knight and said, 'I have seen wounds like this many times. They fester and the leg turns green. The blood is poisoned and the poison kills the patient.'

The knight turned pale. 'Is there nothing you can do to stop this?'

'Only one thing,' the doctor from Europe told him. 'We must cut off the leg before it turns bad!'

'Cut off my leg! the knight moaned. 'I'll never ride or fight again!'

'You'll never ride or fight if you die from the poisoned blood. Make up your mind, man. Lose the leg or lose your life!'

'Then I must lose my leg,' the knight whispered.

The doctor called for a soldier to fetch an axe and he instructed the man where to strike the leg. The Arab doctor turned to me and said, 'This is madness! Can you do nothing to stop him?'

I shook my head. 'They are guests in our country. We must respect their customs.'

The knight turned on his side and I held his arms while the doctor stretched the leg out on a board of wood. When the axe came down the scream of the kight was terrible to hear. 'Again, man! Again!' the doctor from Europe cried, 'You failed to cut through!'

The second blow removed the leg. Blood from the wound soon stopped flowing. Blood does not flow long from corpses. The horror of the operation had killed the man.

The doctor from Europe shrugged his narrow shoulders. 'Ah, well. I had to try. He would have died anyway.' Then he left to practise his brutal skills on some other unlucky patients.

The Arab doctor turned to me and said, 'Such a waste.'

If I am ever wounded in battle then I hope my God lets me be treated by an Arab doctor and not a European butcher.

LITTLE VILLEINS

The Normans ran their countries under a 'feudal system'. Imagine that as a pyramid …

This is the king who sits at the top and owns the lot.

These are the barons who guard the king' s land, and train the men to fight for the king who sits at the top and owns the lot.

These are the knights who look after the villages, and fight for their barons who guard the king's land, and train the men to fight for the king who sits at the top and owns the lot.

These are the villeins who work on the land and work for the knights who look after the villages, who fight for their barons who guard the king's land, and train the men to fight for the king who sits at the top and owns the lot.

These are the serfs who own no land but are owned by the knights who look after the villages, who fight for their barons who guard the king's land, and train the men to fight for the king who sits at the top and owns the lot while they own nothing, not even their bodies.

And lowest of all were the village children – nothing much changes there, then.

Tasks for tots

Was it pleasant being a peasant child? You'd have no school to go to! (So you couldn't learn to read and have the joy of *Horrible Histories* books, of course.)

What would you do all day with no school to imprison and torment you – no sick-making SATs, no dreadful detentions, no rotten reports, no evil essays and hideous homework! Would you be bored without these cool classroom capers?

Of course not! Your parents would find you work as soon as you could walk. Children in Norman times didn't have newspaper rounds and they probably didn't have to keep their bedrooms tidy or help with the washing up. Instead they helped on the land.

WE HAD TO BE IN SCHOOL FOR AN EXTRA 20 MINUTES

I HAD 2 HOURS OF HOMEWORK LAST NIGHT

I'VE GOT TO REVISE DURING THE *HOLIDAYS*

I'VE BEEN WORKING 19 HOURS EVERY DAY SINCE I WAS ONE AND A HALF

You'd have to…

- **collect wood** from the forest for the family fire (but watch out for the big bad wolves and outlaws). Every November villeins (and their children) gathered baskets full of wood for their lord's winter fires. For each basket they gathered he gave them one log!

THIS IS A LOG?

- **collect acorns** and beech nuts from the forest floor in autumn to feed the family pigs. (Then kill and eat the pig in winter and get your own back!)
- **prod the oxen** in the bum with a sharp stick so they'll pull the plough. (But be careful the angry ox doesn't turn and prod you in the bum with its horns.)

I THINK YOUR SHARP STICK IS A LITTLE TOO SHARP

- **turn the grindstone** at harvest time so the men can sharpen their sickles. (Such a boring job you'll be sickle of it in no time.)
- **polish the arrow heads** of your father's arrows using sand (and an arrow strip of cloth).

The good news is the Church banned work on a Sunday. So there's just the chance you may find time to play a game or two…

Games you may want to play

Bubble beaters

Children in Norman times enjoyed blowing bubbles just as children (and some sad grown-ups) do today. The Norman children didn't have plastic loops – they used hollow stalks of straw. Instead of washing-up liquid they'd use Norman bath soap, but it worked the same. If you want to check…

You need:

- a teaspoon of washing-up liquid stirred in half a cup of water
- drinking straws
- a watch with a second hand

To play:

Place one end of a straw in the mixture. Blow gently at the other end till a bubble appears. (Don't suck or you'll end up with the cleanest tonsils in town!)

With two or more players the winner is the one whose bubble lasts longest.

Conkering

William wasn't just a Conqueror. He was a conker-er too! The Normans taught the English the game of conkers. People still play it today – clever kids play conkers but so do adults who take it quite seriously and have a world championship every year! (They're bonkers.) If you care to try it then you will be playing a game about a thousand years old…

You need:
- at least one conker for each player
- string – cut to lengths about half a metre long
- a meat skewer

To make:
Drill a hole through the centre of the conker with the skewer. Push a piece of string through the hole. Tie a knot in the string so the conker can't slip off.

To play:
Toss a coin to decide who goes first. Player 1 swings their string to smash their conker into player 2's. If you hit the conker have another go. (If you miss you don't go again till it's your turn.) Player 2 then has a go at hitting player 1's conker. The first player to shatter the other's conker is the winner.

Punching puppets
Boys dressed in chain-mail coats, carried small lances and shields and played. We don't know what the rules were but

they probably charged at one another the way the grown-ups did on horses. (A point was scored every time a knight shattered his lance on his opponent's shield.) And no doubt there were accidents where smashing shields led to broken noses and splintered lances went into eyes. In other words, nothing too serious and only the odd death here and there.

A much safer game was fighting with puppets. If the weather was bad then the children got out their string puppets. These were about 30 to 40 cm high. The children stood (or knelt) facing one another and pulled the strings to make their puppets fight.

Super skating

In the 1100s William Fitz Stephen wrote about young men skating on the ponds and rivers in winter. If you want to go to your local ice-rink and save on the cost of hiring ice-skates then here's the way to do it ...

You need:

- the shin bones of a sheep or pig (from your local butcher – tell him it's for your poor pooch and he'll give them free!)
- strips of cloth (rip up your bedclothes or a teacher's shirt)
- two broom-handles
- a cushion

196

To make:

Boil the bones in a pot till the flesh drops off and the bones are white and clean. (Add carrots and onions to the water to make soup for when you get home chilled.)

Use strips of cloth to bind the bones to the bottom of your shoes and around your ankles.

Stuff the cushion down the back of your pants. (You'll look stupid but it will stop you getting a bruised and battered bum.)

Sharpen the bottom end of the broom handles and use them to push yourself along (like skis).

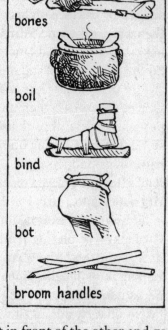

bones

boil

bind

bot

broom handles

To play:

Step on to the ice. Move one foot in front of the other and go as far as you can until you fall flat on your backside.

WHO NEEDS SKATES

Don't ask why anyone would want to do it. People do this at ice rinks all over the country and get a strange twisted pleasure out of it. Some even try it without padding in their pants! Crazy.

197

Normans also enjoyed sledging down hills in snowy weather. Instead of wooden sledges they used a large chunk of ice from a nearby pond. That's an ice way to save money.

Polo

Polo is the sport played on ponies where you try to hit the ball with a stick into a goal. It was invented in Persia around 600 BC and it was meant as a training exercise for horse soldiers. The Muslims were playing it when the Normans arrived in the Holy Land and the Crusaders copied it. Norman boys training to be knights would enjoy it. (Peasants like you and me couldn't afford the horses, of course.) There could be dozens on each side and it was more like war than a ball game.

In Persia the queen and her ladies played it but the Crusaders would never have allowed women to join in. (Probably for the same reason men don't like women to play in their football teams – the men are scared of getting beaten!)

To enjoy this ancient sport today, here's an easy way to do it indoors…

You need:
- a five-a-side football pitch
- hockey sticks
- a tennis ball

To play:
Divide into two equal teams of ten- (or twelve- or fifty-) a-side. Players ride piggy-back on their team-mates. (Switch over when the 'horse' gets tired.) The hockey sticks are used to hit the ball into the opponents' goal. (The sticks must *not* be used to trip opponents' horses, smack opponents in the mouth or to annoy teacher by rattling them up and down wall bars.)

Did you know…?
In China (AD 910) one of the Emperor's favourite relatives was killed playing polo. Emperor A-pao-chi gave the order to have all of the surviving players beheaded.

Games you wouldn't want to play

Slinging scarecrows
Country children acted as killer scarecrows. They didn't just shoo the birds away – they killed the little blighters. Not only did a dead crow leave your parents' precious crops – it could also make a nice snack for dinner.

So learn the Scarecrow song from *The Wizard of Oz* ('If I Only Had a Brain') and get out there and frighten all feathered fiends. Here's how…

You need:
- a bootlace (leather is best)
- a piece of leather about 5 cm square
- a table-tennis ball

To make:
Make a hole at opposite corners of the leather and thread the lace through. Make a loop in one end of the lace and loop it over your forefinger.

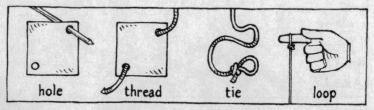

hole   thread   tie   loop

You now have a sling (similar to the one David used to kill Goliath, so be careful how you use it if you meet a giant!).

To shoot:

Place your ammunition (a table-tennis ball) in the leather pad. Hold the free end of the sling between your finger and thumb. Swing it quickly then release the free end of the lace. The ammunition will fly out.

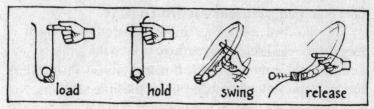

load   hold   swing   release

Note: It takes years of practice to get the action right, let alone hit a target! But don't worry, you have years sitting in freezing fields with nothing else to do. By the time you're grown up you'll be able to hit a tit at twenty paces!

Did you know…?

Stone me, but it's true! The Norman army at the battle of Hastings is remembered for its archers. But the soldiers at the front were armed with slings. They'd have had a pocketful of stones but could always pick up more as they marched forward. Imagine getting one of those in your eye! Not a heroic way to go.

HE'S BEEN PEBBLE-DASHED!

The English fired back with stones attached to pieces of wood – a bit like a stone-age axe!

Scary school

From about the age of seven the sons of Norman lords and knights would train to be knights every afternoon. Good fun, eh? Riding and charging at targets (quintains) with your lance. Sword-fighting and murdering little rabbits and dear deer on hunting expeditions. Great fun!

Now the bad news. Your mornings would be spent in *lessons*. The castle clerks were there to keep the lords' records and keep their money right. But they also had the job of teaching you young knights your lessons.

These lessons were in lovely Latin! Yeuch!

And you don't need me to tell you what that means, do you? You do? Oh, very well. It means. 'Don't despair, have faith in God.' Write it on your next SATs paper and maybe God will give you a helping hand.

The Normans wrote their legal papers in Latin and (when you grew up) you'd have to put your seal on these so it helped if you knew what they meant.

And the really bad news… Each clerk-teacher was armed with a stout stick. No, this wasn't to help him point at the

202

blackboard. It was to whack you across the shoulders if you weren't trying hard enough. And, as a tough little trainee knight you must never cry … or even show that it hurt you!

Chilling childhood

You think your life is hard, perhaps? Just be thankful you didn't grow up like one noble Norman boy. If you went through what he went through then you'd probably end up half crazed with fear. You certainly wouldn't sleep too well at night! Here is his story…

I was just seven years old and starting to train as a knight when my father left home. He was the sixth Duke of Normandy and the only man who could keep the fighting lords from tearing it apart. The country was surrounded by our enemies. Everyone begged my father not to go but he said he wanted to go on a pilgrimage to Monte Gargano. (Some even said he went to beg God to forgive him for killing his own brother!) I never saw him

alive again. He died on his way back —
they say he may have been poisoned.

Before he left father got everyone to
agree that I should be the next duke. I
was left in the care of Count Alan but
he died suddenly.

Count Gilbert took his place — he
lasted a few months before he was
brutally murdered while he was out
riding. They told me Odo the Fat was
the killer.

My tutor Turold died soon after in
the same horrible way.

The head of my household was Osbern
and his death was the most hideous of all.
He was sleeping in my bed-chamber to
protect me from my enemies. I heard
the door open and saw William of
Montgomery slip in. His knife glinted in
the moonlight and before I could cry out
he had slit Osbern's throat.
Poor Osbern's blood lay in a
river over my floor.

Osbern's friends avenged him – they broke into William of Montgomery's house and slew the killer and everyone else they found there. Blood for blood.

My only true friend was my mother's brother, Walter. He slept in my room and if we heard any strange noises at night he would lead me to hide in the only place we felt safe – in the cottages of the poor.

Father, Count Alan, Count Gilbert, Turold and Osbern. All died so that others could control me and so control Normandy.

Brutal and dreadful days. Maybe that's where I learned that the only way to survive was to be violent. To strike anyone who threatened me. Maybe that's where I learned that the law of the Norman duke was simple ... kill or be killed.

Who was the child that had such a grim life before his ninth birthday? William, Duke of Normandy – later called William the Conqueror. Remember that childhood when you look at the ferocious man he grew to be.

MISERABLE MONARCHS

William the Conqueror was a pretty nasty Norman at times. But the Norman kings and queen who followed him could have their nasty moments too…

Red Bill

Name: William II (nicknamed 'Rufus') 1056–1100

Claim to fame: Rufus took over the throne of England from his dad, William the Conqueror. But the Conqueror gave Normandy to one of his other sons, Robert. Rufus went back to Normandy and spent half his time helping Robert to fight the French – and the other half trying to pinch Normandy from him!

Dreadful deeds: Rufus upset everybody and especially the men of the Church. He stole Church lands and Church money and refused to make the popular Anselm the new Archbishop of Canterbury. Then Rufus fell sick. 'You're dying!' the churchmen told him. 'Give us what you want or you will burn in Hell!' Rufus panicked, gave the churchmen what they wanted – then recovered!

Dire death: Rufus went hunting in the New Forest. He fired an arrow at a stag and missed. He then called to a knight, Walter Tirel, 'Shoot!' So Walter shot him … the king, not the stag. Rufus was so unpopular no one blamed Tirel!

YOU KILLED THE KING, YOU SAY? DEAR OH DEAR. STILL, NEVER MIND, WORSE THINGS HAPPEN AT SEA

The king's corpse was loaded on to a cart by some peasants and it's said that blood dripped all the way to Winchester Cathedral where he was buried.

Little Hen

Name: Henry I 1068–1135
Claim to fame: William the Conqueror's youngest son. The first Norman king to be born in England.
Dreadful deeds: Henry was as ruthless as his dad. In 1090 he and his brother Robert went to war against their brother, William II. They captured one of William's knights called Conan and took him up the stairs of their castle tower. Conan begged them for mercy but the brothers just laughed. Henry had a nasty death planned for Conan. He threw him out of the window.

Henry later had trouble with Robert, and ended up locking him away for the rest of his life … and Robert died in his Cardiff Castle prison at the age of 80.

Dire death: Henry's doctor warned him, 'Don't eat those eels, they're bad for you.' Henry ate the eels and had a nasty pain in the gut. The doctor advised, 'What you need is a laxative. It will give you diarrhoea for a day or so but it will clear out your bowels.' Sadly the doctor wasn't a very good doctor. He gave Henry a bit of an overdose. It gave him diarrhoea all right! And it killed him. What a way to go! Pooh!

Sad Steve

Name: Stephen 1097–1154

Claim to fame: Stephen battled for the throne of England with his cousin, Matilda, and brought misery to the whole country.

Dreadful deeds: Before Henry I was dead Stephen swore Henry's daughter (Matilda) could be the next queen of England. What did he do when Henry I died? Grabbed the throne for himself. (That's a bit of a surprise because

Stephen was a good fighter but a bit of a wimp. He was badly bossed about by his mum and his wife. They probably pushed his bum on to the throne of England. This must have been painful because Stephen had a nasty condition called 'piles' which gave him a sore bum.)

COULDN'T I HAVE ANOTHER CUSHION?

Anyway, Matilda was furious and invaded and so it went on. *Dire death:* Stephen, like William the Conqueror, fell ill with a pain in the guts. It was probably a burst appendix. Today that can still kill people but, if they can get to hospital in time, doctors can operate to cut it out. Stephen didn't have any slicing surgeons so he died in agony.

NORMAN NASTINESS

The Normans could be ruthless at times. (And if they set fire to the thatch on your cottage you'd be pretty roofless yourself!)

One of William the Conqueror's cruellest acts was known as 'The Harrying of the North' when he destroyed a whole region. Usually he was merciful to his defeated enemies. What drove him to this awful act?

Evil English in darkest Durham

It would be wrong to think the cruelty was all on the part of the Normans. The English could be pretty nasty when they wanted to be.

Just 60 years before the Battle of Hastings the northerners had beaten the Scots, cut off the best-looking heads and put them on show around the walls of Durham. The message was clear to anyone who wanted to take over – 'Nothing personal, Mr Conqueror. We don't like being ruled by *anybody*!'

In January 1069 the Normans took the city of Durham … for a while. If a monk had kept a personal diary of those dire days in Durham, it might have looked something like this.

> 30th day of January, the year of our Lord one thousand and sixty-nine.
>
> Today I went to the market-place and saw our conquerors. The man Robert of Comines marched into our city at dawn with his army of seven hundred men and put soldiers at every street corner. A few brave men tried to gather and

attack them but they were hacked down by the men in chain armour. The bodies are still in the narrow streets and their blood is trickling towards the River Wear but it is freezing in the gutters before it gets there.

Comines spoke to the crowd – he spoke French, so only a few of us understood. 'I am here by the right of William of Normandy, King of England,' he told us. 'Anyone who refuses to obey an order from me or one of my men will be executed on the spot.' He turned to the Bishop of Durham, Aegelwine, and said, 'Make sure these ignorant English know what I said.'

Our Bishop clutched at his cross and said boldly, 'It will end in your defeat, my lord Comines. You will be thrown out of Durham.'

The Norman sneered and said, 'Talking of being thrown out, I am throwing you out of your palace. It will become my home while I am in Durham. You can sleep in the monastery.'

It is a sad day for Durham. But as we left the market-place we heard the people muttering. A rebel army is already gathering and will attack very soon. As a man of God I hate bloodshed – but the Normans need to be taught a lesson. Let us see what God brings us tomorrow.

—

31st day of January, the year of our Lord one thousand and sixty-nine

Oh the horror and the pity and the glory of it. Early this morning the rebel army arrived and before the Normans were awake they'd broken down our city gates. The people rose to join them armed with sickles and knives. The Normans tried to attack but they were trapped as soon as they entered the narrow city streets.

The Normans were hacked to the ground. The blood of yesterday's dead English was washed away by the blood of the Norman soldiers. When the Normans saw what was happening some fled to join Robert Comines in the Bishop's palace. But the mob set fire to the house.

'You'll set fire to our church!' I tried to tell them as the flames blew towards the Minster. Then God showed his glory as the wind changed and saved our lovely building. A miracle of God!

But nothing could save Comines and his cut-throat killers. They burned to death and I still hear their screams in my mind. But it is silent out there now. A light snow is falling to cover the Norman bodies.

Every last Norman is dead. Tonight we will pray that they never return.

In fact just two Norman soldiers managed to escape and take the shocking news back to William the Conqueror.

He was not pleased. Not one bit.

The magical mist

Of course the Normans *did* return, but again they failed to take Durham. This time the people of the city believed they were saved by a miracle…

15th day of September, the year of our Lord one thousand and sixty-nine

Since those blood-soaked days of January we have been steeling ourselves for the return of Duke William's armies. Messengers arrived three days ago to say they had set off from York and probably arrive today. All of yesterday we prayed in the Minster for God to spare us and today we heard our prayers have been answered.

A rider clattered into the market-place on his sweating horse, demanding to be taken to the bishop. I was sure that the news would be bad but I led him up the steep streets to the bishop's new house. I led the man in to Bishop Aegelwine and you cannot blame me if I stayed a little while to hear the news.

'Bishop,' the man cried. 'It's a miracle! The

Norman army reached Northallerton, barely a day's march from Durham, and they've turned back!'

The bishop nodded but argued, 'That is no miracle, my son.'

'But it is! As they set off a sudden fog descended on them from heaven. The Normans could not see the road ahead of them. They were terrified. They were sure that it was a sign.'

I hurried from the room with the news for my brothers who were in the Minster. I rested my hand on the coffin of our dear Saint Cuthbert and felt it chilly and damp as if it were covered in a mist. 'Saint Cuthbert has saved us!' I told them. 'Saint Cuthbert has sent a fog to confuse our enemies! We are saved!'

And today the word has spread through Durham. We have been saved by Cuthbert's miracle.

The truth is never that simple. A Danish army had landed on the coast just as the Normans set off from York to march on Durham. That was the *real* reason the Norman army turned back. The invasion had to be dealt with first.

The miraculous path

The people and the monks of Durham may have believed the miracle of Saint Cuthbert. But they were still sure the Normans would be back – and that their first victim would be the corpse of old Saint Cuthbert in Durham Minster.

So the monks decided to move the coffin further north to the safety of the island of Lindisfarne. The island is just off the Northumberland coast and when the monks arrived they could find no boat to take them across.

Then they looked in amazement as the waters fell away and a path appeared. It let them walk all the way to the island. The monks cried...

ANOTHER ONE OF SAINT CUTHBERT'S MIRACLES!

The truth is this path appears twice a day, every day, when the tide goes out!

The monks left the coffin in safety and returned to Durham and a nasty shock – their Bishop Aegelwine had run away and taken some of Durham's richest treasures with him!

CHEEKY MONKY

Wise man, Aegelwine. He knew that this time the Normans would return and take their revenge. He didn't want to be around when they did. They were about to begin...

The Harrying of the North

Some of the stories told about the Normans show that wherever they went the message was, 'You don't mess with a Norman'.

The Norman invasion of England in 1066 didn't put William's bum safely on the throne. The English weren't going to give up just because King Harold had been hacked at Hastings.

In 1069 the English revolted in the south while the warrior-leader Edric the Wild went wild in the west. In the north the Vikings crossed the North Sea to help Saxon Prince Edgar.

AND US NORTHERNERS WERE SO PLEASED TO SEE THEM WE JOINED OUR FRIENDS THE VIKINGS!

WE ARE A VERY FRIENDLY PEOPLE!

The Vikings marched on York. The Norman defenders set fire to the city and left the safety of York castle to fight the enemy in open battle. They were wiped out...

THE ONLY GOOD NORMAN IS A DEAD ONE, AS MY OLD DAD USED TO SAY

ACTUALLY HIS DAD USED TO SAY THAT ABOUT US VIKINGS!

The northern English towns and villages held fine fat feasts for the vicious Vikings. There were rumbles of rebellion in the rest of England.

William set off to sort out the nuisance in the north. He didn't just want to win. He wanted to destroy them so completely they would never rebel again. What he did became known as 'The Harrying of the North'.

The Vikings left York before William could catch them…

William set about destroying the northern region as he marched through it. Every English male was murdered.

The houses and the barns were burned. The farm animals were killed so there was nothing left for the people to eat.

Corpses were left to rot by the side of the roads and the desperate English survivors ate them to stay alive…

Horrible Histories Health Warning: Eating dead bodies you find in a ditch can damage your health. So don't do it.

Disease came along to add to the misery of the survivors. The northern towns and villages were still struggling to recover years later.

The North certainly didn't revolt again. The Conqueror's cruelty worked.

Twenty years after 'The Harrying of the North' William the Conqueror started to feel bad about his cruelty. It's said he was dead sorry … unlike the English who were simply dead dead.

The stuffed saint
When the Norman kingdom had settled, over 30 years later, they brought Cuthbert back to Durham to put him in the new cathedral the Normans were building there.

Before the body was moved to its new resting place the coffin was opened by ten monks. They reported that the body had not rotted and it smelled sweet!

It was 417 years old! Bet you don't look fresh and smell sweet when you're 417 years old!

A miracle? Or was the body mummified when it was first buried? Was the sweet smell the scent of the oils used?

The coffin can still be seen in Durham Cathedral today. But a) do not try to get into Cuth's coffin for a quick peek, and b) do not pour oil over your favourite granny in the hope she'll stay fresh for another 417 years!

Cuthbert appeared to have forgiven the Normans for disturbing his rest. There is a story that at the end of the 1100s the Norman Archbishop of York was seriously ill. The doctors said there was nothing they could do for him. Then he had a dream in which he was told to go to the tomb of Saint Cuthbert and sleep there. The Archbish did as he was told and ... Lo! He had a vision that old Cuth appeared and ran his hands over him. The Norman was cured immediately.

(Please note, that archbishop is now dead and has been for 800 years. Cuth's cure works once but you can't expect him to keep you going for ever.)

Whacking Walcher

The Normans gave all the top jobs in England to Norman lords. In the north the Bishop of Durham became a prince as well as a bishop. He ruled the church and the people.

The first Norman prince-bishop of Durham was William Walcher. It wasn't an easy job. English monks from a Tyneside monastery at Jarrow had to pick up the pieces of Walcher's last quarrel. If one of the young monks had written home, his letter may have described the event something like this…

16 May 1080

Dear Mum and Dad,

You never told me it was going to be so dangerous when you sent me to be a monk! Can't I come home now and work on the farm? I was in Gateshead this morning and you should see the mess! It was enough to make me sick. Far worse than slaughter-time on the farm each autumn. Let me tell you about it and then you can see why I want to come home.

You may remember Bishop Walcher was getting on quite well. He'd made a lot of friends with the great English families around here. And one of his best pals was Liulf of Lumley. Of course there were people jealous of Liulf weren't there? The ones who were most jealous were the bishop's own Norman friends. Especially that Gilbert!

That Gilbert was a monster! Worse

than William the Conqueror! You may have heard that Gilbert was so jealous of Liulf of Lumley he set off for the Lumley house and murdered him in his bed. Then he went off and tried to kill all of the rest of the Lumley family in their beds! He was wild as a fox in a chicken run.

Everybody blamed Bishop Walcher, didn't they? Gilbert was the bishop's man. There were riots up in Gateshead when the English heard about the Lumley murders. So the brave bishop said, 'Look, I'll come to a meeting with the Lumley family and make peace.'

'Yeah,' the Lumley family said. 'And make sure you bring your friend Gilbert with you!'

So off he went to Gateshead church. Naturally he had a hundred guards with him, but it didn't do him much good. You can imagine the mob that met them at the church! 'Kill the bishop! Kill the bishop!' they chanted.

Well, poor old Walcher fled into the church. But the mob forced him to send Gilbert outside to make peace. Make peace! They made pieces! Pieces of Gilbert! Bits of him in every corner of the churchyard.

And that's when they set fire to the church. The bishop staggered out, choking with the smoke. They say his eyes were so blinded by the smoke he couldn't see. Just as well, I suppose. Everybody in that English mob wanted to have a chop at him. He was a real mess.

I know this, Dad, because they sent us from Jarrow this morning to tidy up and give Walcher a Christian burial. We found his body, stripped of its prince-bishop robes, and we could hardly recognize it. Like I say, a real mess. We had to pick it up, put it on a cart and take it back with us.

A few of the mob came back to the ruined church and pelted us with mud. 'Let the crows have him!' they told us. I tell you, Dad and Mum, I've never been so scared in my life!

They say the murderers have fled to Scotland. But I can't do that, can I? Please can I come home?

Your loving son, Eadulf

Cropped coast

In 1085 William the Conqueror was back in Normandy when news arrived – England was about to be invaded. King Cnut of Denmark was teaming up with his son-in-law, Robert of Flanders. Together they'd fight for the English throne that Cnut believed should be his.

William gathered a huge army and shipped it across the English Channel. Reports at the time were sensational...

READ ALL ABAHT IT! CHANNEL FILLED WITH SHIPS THAT STRETCH FROM THE ENGLISH COAST TO THE NORMANDY COAST! READ ALL ABAHT IT!

NORMAN NEWS – SHIPS SHORE TO SHORE

William wasn't sure where Cnut would land. He knew that an invading army could survive by looting the farms on the coast. So what did he do?

Answer: William ordered that all the crops and stores of food along the English coast should be destroyed. The poor people who'd worked hard all year were moved inland for safety. The invasion never arrived so those farmers moved back to their homes by the coast ... and hunger.

Caught red-handed

Bishop Odo of Bayeux was William the Conqueror's half-brother. In conquered England he acted as a judge and, with the help of a jury, decided arguments.

Being a member of a jury today means you have to be fair and honest. If you're not then you could go to prison. But prison isn't as bad as the punishment Odo saved for cheating jurymen in his day.

If there had been newspapers in Norman times then the case may have been reported like this …

English edition   Price: Half a dozen eggs

THE NORMAN NEWS

Jury Fury

Angry Odo

Bishop Odo gave the punishers some punishment today … and it didn't half hurt! Twelve members of the jury in the Islesham Manor Case have been found guilty of lying in court. Our readers will remember the case where the Bishop of Rochester and the Sheriff of Cambridge were arguing over who owned the stately home. The twelve good men and untrue of the jury decided to give it to the Sheriff.

That might have been an end to it but a Rochester monk made a sensational claim. The jury had not played fair, and, what's more, the mean monk could prove it!

225

Today Bishop Odo (The Basher Bishop, or Bish Bash as our readers know him) heard the evidence and decided the jury were indeed as bent as a nine-groat piece. First Bish Bash fined them till their purses were empty as Harold's eye-socket. Then he ordered that the guilty men should have their right hands plunged into boiling water.

Our ace reporter, Hugh Je Scoop, watched the sentence being carried out. 'I'd like to get my hand on the monk that fingered me,' muttered one victim (who wishes to remain nameless).

Juror in hot water

His wife Jeanne de Yorke (who also wishes to remain nameless) said, 'I told him that trying his hand at lying to Odo would get him in hot water. Once Odo takes matters in hand he always wins hands down. You have to hand it to him. Wasn't I right?'

NORMAN ITALY

The Norman control of Italy began almost by accident, probably around the year 999. Forty Norman pilgrims were returning from Jerusalem to Normandy and rested at Salerno in Southern Italy. While they were there the town was raided by Saracens. The Normans were shocked to see that the Salerno citizens did little to stop them.

The Normans went to Prince Gaimar of Salerno and said: 'Give us horses and weapons and we'll sort out these Saracens for you!'

The Normans drove the Saracens away and the prince was delighted. Prince Gaimar begged them to stay but they refused. The prince loaded them with gifts and sent more gifts back to Normandy to persuade other Normans to return. Prince Gaimar's message was:

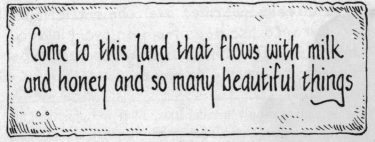

Come to this land that flows with milk and honey and so many beautiful things

Normans knights returned to Italy and set about the invaders from all sides. They drove Greek invaders from Apulia in the south-west of Italy. But which were worse for

227

the Italians? Their Greek enemies or Norman 'friends'? As William of Apulia said at the time…

All the people of Apulia feared the Normans and many perished as the victims of their cruelty

WHO ARE WE HARASSING TODAY?

DOES IT MATTER?

That's the Normans for you! Invite them in to help and they boss you about and beat you up. It's a bit like having burglars in your home and inviting bullies in to bash the burglars.

The Normans won five great victories in a row. But once the Greeks realized the power of the Normans they returned with a huge army to oppose them. The historian Amatus said…

> October 1018
> The Greeks swarmed over the battlefield of Ofanto like bees from an overflowing hive. Of 250 Normans only ten survived, the rest were cut to pieces.

The Normans didn't 'invade' Italy. They were just knights looking for a good fight. They'd fight for anybody who paid them. Some even joined the Greeks and fought against Normans who were on the side of Apulia. (At least they were kind to their Norman opponents when they defeated them!)

The heroic Hautevilles

And then along came the Hauteville brothers – all twelve of them. Once these battling boys arrived then the Normans started to take over southern Italy.

The Normans seemed to be outnumbered in every battle they fought, yet they always won. Sometimes they avoided fighting against huge numbers. Young William, for example, challenged the enemy leader to 'single combat' – one against one, a bit like a tennis match at Wimbledon only with a bit more blood.

WILLIAM KNOCKED THE EMIR OFF HIS HORSE THEN SLEW HIM. ....

A KNIGHT'S GOTTA DO WHAT A KNIGHT'S GOTTA DO!

FOR THAT GREAT DEED THE KNIGHT BECAME KNOWN AS WILLIAM IRON ARM.

AND MY HEAD IS PRETTY HARD TOO!

And remember when the Normans were massacred at Ofanto by the buzzing-bee Greeks? William Iron Arm went back to the same battlefield 23 years later (1041 if you're a dummy at summies). They say William Iron Arm had a terrible fever at the time but he won this return match.

CRAZY CRUSADERS

In 1096 the Pope asked Christians to go and capture the Holy Land from the Muslims. Of course the Normans were the first to join in. They'd had plenty of practice fighting Muslims in Italy. Now they had another excuse for a good fight.

Many knights fought in the Crusades because they were Christians or because they were serving their lord. But some knights were 'mercenary' and fought because they were paid to fight – 800 hyperperes for a knight and 400 for his squire. These mercenary knights had to work for their pay – or else. The punishment for a knight without fight could be to have his armour taken away. Still, that was better than being a cowardly ordinary soldier. He would have his hand pierced with a hot iron.

Did you know… ?
Knightly Norman William de Perci had Whitby Abbey built. He then went off on Crusade, where he died. It is said his

heart was brought back for burial at Whitby Abbey. Of course Whitby is where Count Dracula was later said to have arrived in England to go in search of fresh victims. Wonder if he had a munch on de Perci's blood pump?

231

Powerful Prester

In 1145 a bishop of Syria wrote a startling letter to the Pope…

Your Holiness,

I have wonderful news for your brave Crusaders. There are many Muslim states between you and the Holy Land. But there is one mighty Christian state beyond Persia which may well come to the aid of the Crusaders.

This state is ruled by a priest-king called Prester John. Prester John is a descendant of the three wise men who took gifts to the baby Jesus.

Prester John has already defeated the Muslims in Persia and his armies are heading towards us. Let us pray that he arrives in time to help our brave knights.

The Bishop of Syria

When the news reached the Pope, the Crusaders became excited by the idea of having such a powerful ally – even though no one had heard of him before 1145! The excitement grew when a letter arrived from Prester John himself.

The letter was a forgery – Prester John didn't exist!

Imagine you were the Pope and you received a letter which said…

Your Holiness

I am Prester John and I rule the lands beyond Persia. I try to rule as a good Christian even though I am the most powerful king on earth. I have seventy-two lesser kings who accept me as their leader.

My lands are so rich that there are no poor people in them. There is no lying, no stealing, no crime of any kind. Still, I do have a magical mirror in my palace and through it I can look into any part of my country. If there is any plotting going on then I know all about it.

I have magical jewels that can control how warm or cold the weather is and a church which can grow or shrink depending on how many people are in it.

I look foward to the day when you can visit my land and see these wonders and many more.

Your loyal Christian friend

Prester John.

Now, if you'd been the Pope you would take one look at the letter, say, 'Ho! Ho! Very funny!' and drop it into the nearest bin.

What did Pope Alexander III do? He wrote back to Prester John! This is a bit like writing to Father Christmas … very nice for five-year-old children to believe. But the leader of the Western Christian Church? What a Popish plonker!

The seriously bad news was that an Eastern invader had indeed defeated the Muslims in Persia in the 1140s. But it wasn't a mighty Christian priest-king called Prester John. It was the ruthless Mongol warlord Kor-Khan and the coming of the Mongols was *not* good news for the Christians of Europe.

Gorgeous Saint George

Saint George was a hero to the Normans. Why? Because he was a great fighter, of course. The Normans loved fighters.

St George was also a Christian who died because of his faith. The Normans believed that anyone who died for being a Christian would go straight to heaven – that's why they were so eager to fight in the Crusades against the Muslims.

So, who was this St George and what happened to him? It's pretty gruesome, but it may be worth it to get that top spot up in heaven…

How to become a saint

In the AD 500s George had been a brilliant Roman soldier. He became a Christian and gave all his money away to the poor. When the Emperor Diocletian decided to exterminate the Christians, George was tortured.

Do you have a teacher for Religious Education? Do you

have a local vicar or priest? Do you even have someone in your class who is so good and holy they make you sick? Then this is your chance to do them a favour and make them a saint. All you have to do is copy what the Romans did to St George.

Make your own saint

For this you need a really holy person and a lot of patience.

1. First lay your saint on the ground. Cover her/him with stones then larger rocks and finally get a few little boulders and pile them on until s/he is crushed. If your saint is truly a saint then s/he will survive. So…

2. Take a wheel covered in spikes and roll it to the top of a steep hill. Tie your saint to the wheel and roll it down the hill. Just like Jack and Jill but a bit bloodier. If your saint is truly a saint then s/he will survive. So…

3. Take a pair of iron shoes and heat them till they are red hot. Put them on the feet of your saint and set her/him off to run in them. They'll set off hot foot, you can be sure. If your saint is truly a saint then s/he will survive. So…

4. Tie your saint to a cross, facing the cross. Take leather whips with knots in the end and a team of whippers. Whip the saint till their skin is hanging off their body. If your saint is truly a saint then s/he will survive. So…

5. Dig a deep pit in the ground. Throw your saint into the pit and cover her/him with quicklime (calcium oxide if you want the posh word). This will burn off their flesh till they're skinny as a skeleton key. If your saint is truly a saint then s/he will survive. So…

6. Get a bottle of poison at your local chemist shop. Slip the poison into your saint's tea and watch them drink the poison. If your saint is truly a saint then s/he will survive. So…

7. Behead your saint. That's what Diocletian did and it finally killed off Georgie.

But before he died – and in between the tortures – George…

- chatted to an angel
- raised dozens of people from the dead
- raised an ox from the dead
- converted the Emperor's wife to Christianity (she got the chop too, by the way!)
- converted 40,900 other people
- had the Emperor carried away by a whirlwind of fire

Whatever happened to the dragon?

Bet you thought Saint George was a saint because he slew a dragon? The Saint George that the Normans loved never did that. The dragon only appears in the book *Golden Legend*, written in the late 1200s. So now you know.

Horrible for horses

Life in the Norman world could be awful for horses. Especially when they went into battle…

- The charge of Norman knights was a fearsome thing, but the Muslim warriors found a way to stop it. They used their arrows and javelins to bring down the horses. Once the horse fell then the knight could be battered senseless.

One knight, de Joinville, was hit by five arrows – but his poor horse was hit by 15 and fell. Later that year de Joinville had a spear thrust through his leg. It also stuck firmly in the neck of his horse and pinned him there. This was a bit of a pain in the neck for both of them!

- An Italian historian, Amatus, described a Norman duke as follows…

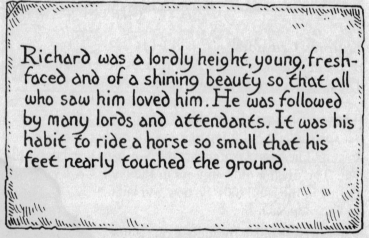

'All who saw him loved him'? I'll bet the little horses in Italy didn't love him! 'Oh, no!' they must have whinnied when they saw him coming. 'Why can't he pick on some horse his own size?'

- Horses are reasonable swimmers. They can even swim with a rider on their back. But it's a bit much to ask a horse to swim with a heavy war saddle and a rider with chain-mail armour, iron helmet and battle sword. That's what the knights expected from their horses after the battle of Val-es-Dunes in 1047. Not only did the riders drown (which served them right) but they took the poor horses down with them. A writer who visited the battlefield said…

The water-mills of Borbillon had their wheels clogged with the bodies.

Crummy Crusades

By the middle of the 1200s the Crusades were not so popular. The religious writer, Humbert of Romans, said…

Priests who call for a Crusade are mocked these days. And the knights who sign up to go are usually drunk at the time!

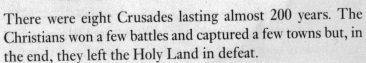

There were eight Crusades lasting almost 200 years. The Christians won a few battles and captured a few towns but, in the end, they left the Holy Land in defeat.

Still, the Normans got most of what they wanted from the Crusades – an exciting punch-up, a bit of glory … and a ticket to their Christian heaven. What more would a Norman knight need?

MISCHIEVOUS MONKS

The Normans set up hundreds of monasteries wherever they went in Normandy, Italy, the Holy Land and England. Men and women flocked to become monks and nuns, but not every one was a saint – not every religious place was holy.

Wholly holy

Abbot Ailred was in charge of Rievaulx Abbey in Yorkshire (founded in 1131). When he died monks wrote his story and didn't forget to praise themselves!

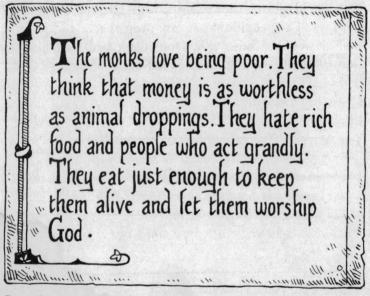

The monks love being poor. They think that money is as worthless as animal droppings. They hate rich food and people who act grandly. They eat just enough to keep them alive and let them worship God.

Sounds a pretty boring sort of life really. But of course not all monks were as goody-goody as that …

Not wholly holy

Gerald of Wales (1146–1223) said that the monasteries could be very ungodly places.

240

1 Wealth

They got lands by acting like saints and using 'God' as every other word.

So, the monks just *appeared* to be holy so they could get their hands on lands.

Interesting thought, using 'God' as every other word! That would mean if they read the Ruth chapter of the Bible that says 'Thy people shall be my people, and thy God my God', it would become: 'Thy God people God shall God be God my God people God and God thy God God God my God God God.'

2 Land

Once they get land they waste no time in putting it to use. The woods are cut down and levelled into a plain, bushes give way to barley and willows to wheat. They flatten villages, overthrow churches, turn villagers on to the roads and don't hesitate to cast down altars and level all under the plough.

I CAN FLATTEN ANYTHING. I'VE GOT A BULLDOZER

THAT'S NOTHING, I'VE GOT A MONASTERY

Gerald went on to say that if a man invited the monks on to part of his land, they ended up throwing him out of the rest. 'The coming of Cistercian monks is worse than the coming of a war.' Today he might have said a bit like motorway builders – except he isn't alive today and the Normans didn't have motorways.

3 Ruthlessness

The most amazing story was of a knight who refused to give up his land to the monks of Byland Abbey. Walter Map, a Welsh writer of the time, described what happened next...

> *One night they entered his house with masks over their faces, armed with swords and spears, and they murdered him and his family. When his relations arrived three days later they found the houses and barns had all disappeared and in their place was a well-ploughed field.*

BYLAND ABBEY?

THIEVELAND ABBEY, MORE LIKE!

Sort of, 'Night-night, knight!'

4 Simple food

Then there was the rule that the monks should eat simple food and be silent during meals. If they wanted to ask for salt or water then they used one of the hundred signs they had.

St Bernard of Clairvaux was horrified by what he saw at Canterbury…

> *As to the dishes and the number of them – what shall I say? I have often heard sixteen or more costly dishes were placed on the table. Many kinds of fish (roast and boiled, stuffed and fried) many dishes created with eggs and pepper by skilful cooks and so on! The meal was washed down with wine, claret, mead and all drinks that can make a man drunk. The rule of silence did not prevent monks from showing their pleasure with signs that made them look more like jesters or clowns than monks. They were all waving with fingers, hands and arms and whistling to one another instead of speaking.*

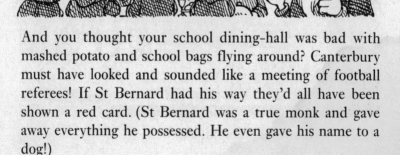

And you thought your school dining-hall was bad with mashed potato and school bags flying around? Canterbury must have looked and sounded like a meeting of football referees! If St Bernard had his way they'd all have been shown a red card. (St Bernard was a true monk and gave away everything he possessed. He even gave his name to a dog!)

5 Little food

Not all monks got away with this good living. Gerald of Wales tells of the monks of St Swithuns, Winchester…

The monks had a good excuse for having so much food. They said they gave away their left-over food to the poor. The more dishes the monks were given the more scraps there were for the poor!

Nice try, boys.

Horrible Histories Health Warning: Do not believe everything you read in history books. Gerald of Wales twice applied to become Bishop of St David's in Wales. In both cases the monks persuaded the king not to give Gerald the job. In both cases the job went to a monk. Gerald had good reason to hate monks. His stories must have been written with a bit of spite.

6 Women

The Bible says, 'All wickedness is little compared to the wickedness of a woman.' (Female readers, don't write and complain to me. I didn't say it. Write to God.) Monks were expected to keep away from them.

Now if you are a monk then there is one sure way to lose interest in women. Don't let your naughty bits get over-heated. How do you keep them cool? Do not wear any underpants. And good Cistercian monks wore no underpants.

But this created other problems. One day King Henry II was riding through a town when a Cistercian monk stumbled, trying to get out of his way. The monk fell flat on his face and his robe blew over his head. The king said nothing but a priest who was riding with the king said…

Cursed be the Cistercians who show their backsides.

No doubt the monk's cheeks turned red with embarrassment … the cheeks of his face, of course. What did you think I meant?

Did you know…?
When a boy joined a monastery at the age of seven he was given a monk's robes and a monk's hair cut. But there was

245

one thing he didn't get until he became an adult monk at the age of 16. What was it?

Gerry's Welsh wonder

Gerald of Wales wrote a book about his travels through Wales in 1188. He tells a story that probably doesn't belong in a travel book...

nce upon a time there was a Welsh boy called Eliodorus who used to visit the kingdom of the dwarfs, deep underground. He played with a dwarf prince and their favourite game was playing with a golden ball. One day Eliodorus tried to steal the golden ball. When the dwarf king found out he was furious. From that day on the gateway to the kingdom of the dwarfs was forever closed to the boy. Eliodorus grew up to be a priest while the dwarf prince lived happily ever under.

Yes, Gerald, and there are fairies at the bottom of our garden.

NORMAN QUIZ

1 A knight who upset his leader could be punished with his own horse. How?

a) He was forced to trot along a road in full armour on his horse.

b) He was tied to the tail of the horse and had to run behind it or be dragged.

c) He was forced to eat it … raw … without salt, pepper or mustard. Not even a cup of tea to wash it down with.

I THINK THAT ONE'S A BIT TOO RAW

BAP!

CRASH!

2 Normans were Western Christians and during the Crusades they met Eastern Christians. Crusaders were discouraged from marrying Eastern Christian women. What happened to them if they did?

a) They were banished to the desert with just a camel for company.

b) They lost their armour which was melted down.

c) They lost the lands they owned back home.

3 The Scots did a sword dance – skipping quickly over sharp swords. What did the English dance over?

a) Smouldering coals.

b) Eggs.

c) Slithering snakes.

OI! WATCH IT, TWINKLE TOES!

4 Crusaders faced a dreadful weapon in the Middle East: 'Greek Fire'. It caught alight as soon as it touched sea water and threatened their ships. How did Norman crusaders fight Greek Fire?

a) With pee.

b) With spit.

c) They dialled 999 and let the Phrygian Fire-fighters fight it.

5 What was the Norman punishment for murder?

a) Hanging by the neck till dead.

b) Having your eyes put out.

c) Beheading (with a blunt axe).

6 Saint Godric died in 1170 at the age of 105. What did he do before he became a hermit monk and a saintly man?

a) He was a pie seller.

b) He was a pirate.

c) He was a pilot.

WHAT DO YOU THINK OF THE PIE?

I THINK YOU SHOULD GIVE UP PIES AND BECOME A HERMIT MONK AND A SAINTLY MAN

7 William the Conqueror knew he was dying in 1087, so he left his kingdom to…

a) His wife – but he was so ill he'd forgotten she was dead.

b) His son William Rufus (who became William II).

c) God.

8 What was the first thing William did when he jumped ashore at Hastings?

a) Fell flat on his face.

b) Fell down on his knees to pray.

c) Fell about laughing when he heard King Harold was 300 miles away.

9 Abbot Thurstan became the new Norman boss at Glastonbury but upset the monks there. The monks argued with Thurstan. What did he do?

a) He was so upset he jumped off the bell tower to his death.

b) He sent in Norman soldiers to slit a few monks' throats.

c) He prayed for a miracle and God sent angels to talk to the monks.

10 A Norman knight swore to prove his love for a lady. She told him to go off and pick up all the stones on the beaches of Brittany. What did he do?

a) Collected an army to do the job and won the heart of the lady.

b) Tried to do it himself but hurt his back and never fought again.

c) Sulked and went to bed for two years.

fig 1. a dark knight

Answers:

1 a) Trotting on a war-horse in full armour was painful. Knights walked to the battlefield and then set off at a canter into the charge. And they didn't gallop into the charge (the way you see in films). Some horses would go faster than others and the line would not be straight. The idea was to hit the enemy as a single block – a bit like the charge of pupils from the school gates at holiday time!

2 c) This didn't happen to all Norman knights but generally it was a bad idea to fall for an Eastern Christian woman, even if she was as pretty as a pot-bellied pig. Still, it could have been worse. A Greek knight who married an Eastern Christian woman could lose a hand or a foot.

3 b) The English danced over eggs. Not so brave as the Scots – unless there's a very angry hen in the room. You may like to try this in the kitchen. Place half a dozen eggs on the floor, turn on the radio and dance around. Too easy, you say? Fine! Try it blindfolded.

4 a) The recipe for Greek Fire has been lost since it was used in the Middle Ages. We can't test the fire-fighting methods to see if they'd work. But the Normans *believed* that throwing sand over the Greek Fire or pouring pee on it was the best way to kill the flames. That is not to say they stood there and risked singeing their piddling bits. If they expected an attack of Greek Fire they'd collect barrels of the stuff. Let's hope they didn't mix them up with the wine barrels.

5 b) The Normans were cruel but they rarely gave the death sentence to criminals. Prison was only used to hold criminals until their trial. A murderer might lose his hands or his eyes. Having your eyes put out was also the punishment for killing one of William the Conqueror's deer. Does that mean a human life was worth no more than the life of a deer?

6 b) Godric was born in Norfolk the year before William the Conqueror invaded. He grew up to be a pedlar – a sort of travelling salesman. Then he became a sea pirate. When his voyages took him as a pilgrim to Compostella in Spain he saw how wicked he'd been. 'I don't want to join a monastery,' he decided. 'I want to live a holy life alone … as a hermit.' He had a fun life in a cave but was driven out by wolves. He finally settled into a specially built hermitage that the Normans built for him. See? You too can have a specially built council house if you're a good boy.

7 c) William hadn't inherited the crown of England from a father who had been king before him, so people could argue that there was no reason why his son should become the new king. Also he'd taken it in battle with a lot of blood spilt. That wouldn't look too good when he arrived at the gates of Heaven, would it?

'What have you done on earth, William?'

'Caused a few thousand bloody deaths!'

'Then go to hell!'

So William said, 'I leave my kingdom to God ... and I hope God will give it to my second son, William.'

God didn't appear to argue.

8 a) William landed and stumbled. 'Ooooh!' his followers gasped. 'That's a bad sign!' But clever Will grabbed a handful of sand and said, 'See! I've already seized Harold's land!'

LOOKS LIKE HE'S EATEN A BIT TOO

9 b) Thurstan sent for soldiers so the monks locked themselves in the monastery church. The soldiers easily broke down the door. Three of the monks rushed to the altar to pray – that didn't alter their fate. They were hacked to death. Many of the other monks were wounded as the soldiers lashed out.

10 c) The knight had asked for it really. Never ask a lady, 'What can I do to win your love?' She may not want her love to be won and might set an impossible task! It's much more simple to say, 'Do you fancy going to the pictures with me?'

EPILOGUE

The fashion at the first millennium was for men to have hair to their shoulders and long moustaches. The Normans cut their hair short and shaved their faces (except the women who didn't cut their hair short or shave their faces). To their enemies the Normans must have looked like skinheads!

And they behaved like skinheads too. They got what they wanted by being violent and they grew to enjoy fighting. (This was before television was invented, so they had to do something to pass the time.)

Of course the Normans had the perfect excuse ...

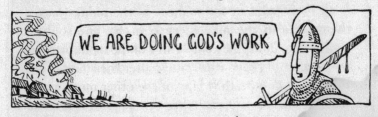

You may like to try this excuse some time ...

Of course you might be punished! Most people believe we should stand up to bullies like the Normans. (So, in 1999, when Serb bullies barged into Kosovo other countries joined forces to stop them.)

The Normans, like their Viking ancestors, were fearless fighters. They charged around Europe and changed it for ever. Why did they do it?

Italian historian Geoffrey Malaterra said…

> *They are passionate about wealth and power, yet they despise it when they have it. They are always looking for more.*

Greedy, nasty Normans.

English Historian William of Malmesbury summed them up like this…

> *They are proudly dressed and delicate about their food – but not too much. They are jealous of their equals – and always want to do better than their superiors. They rob their subjects – yet they defend them against others. They are faithful to their lords – yet the slightest insult makes them wicked. They are only treacherous when they think they can get away with it.*

They probably weren't nice to know, but they were the sort of people who would survive in today's world.

But did the Normans really win?

When French King Philip II took Normandy in 1204, the Normans in England had to choose – should they stay and become English? Or join the French to keep their Norman lands but lose their English ones? They stayed in England.

Some historians say this means the English won – the English didn't become Normans – the Normans became English!

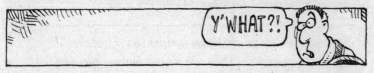

It's a horrible historical world where winners are losers and losers end up winners.

Horrible Histories:
The Savage Stone Age
The Awesome Egyptians
The Groovy Greeks
The Rotten Romans
The Ruthless Romans
The Cut-throat Celts
The Smashing Saxons
The Vicious Vikings
The Stormin' Normans
The Angry Aztecs
The Incredible Incas
The Measly Middle Ages
The Terrible Tudors
Even More Terrible Tudors
The Slimy Stuarts
The Gorgeous Georgians
The Vile Victorians
The Villainous Victorians
The Barmy British Empire
The Frightful First World War
The Woeful Second World War
The Blitzed Brits
Loathsome London

Horrible Histories Specials:
Bloody Scotland
Cruel Kings and Mean Queens
Dark Knights and Dingy Castles
England
France
Ireland
Rotten Rulers
Rowdy Revolutions
The 20th Century
The USA
Wicked Words

Also available:
Cruel Crime and Painful Punishment
Dreadful Diary
Horrible Christmas
The Mad Miscellany
The Wicked History of the World